CW00591772

JOYCE COUNTY

First published in 2016 by Currach Press
55A Spruce Avenue, Stillorgan Industrial Park
Blackrock, Co. Dublin
www.currach.ie

Copyright © 2016 Ray Burke

All rights reserved. Without limiting the rights under copyright reserved
alone, no part of this publication may be reproduced, stored in or
introduced into a retrieval system, or transmitted, in any form or by any
means (electronic, mechanical, photocopying, recording or otherwise)
without the prior written permission of both the copyright owner and the
above publisher of the book.

ISBN: 978-1-78218-885-8

Set in Freight Text Pro 10/14
Cover and book design by Helene Pertl | Currach Press
Printed by Bell & Bain Ltd

Cover reproduction of 'She Weeps Over Rahoon' in Joyce's own
handwriting, with a decorative initial capital letter by his daughter Lucia,
is from a limited edition facsimile that Joyce presented to NUI Galway in
1935 and is reproduced with the kind permission of NUI Galway.

JOYCE COUNTY

Galway and James Joyce
by Ray Burke

CURRACH PRESS

DUBLIN

*For the Burkes and McDermotts of Galway and Oranmore,
all the living and the dead.*

In Galway, as in China, the dead are more important than the living, so that a friendly reminiscence is enough to recall them from oblivion.

— Oliver St John Gogarty, *Rolling Down the Lea*

All men owe honour to the poets – honour
and awe, for they are dearest to the Muse
who puts upon their lips the ways of life.

— Homer, *The Odyssey*, Book VIII, line 512

CONTENTS

INTRODUCTION

Galway is next to Dublin as the most important place in the writings of James Joyce. His foremost heroines are based on his wife and muse, Nora Barnacle, who came from Galway city. He wrote poetry and prose about Galway and he wrote memorably and at length about his visits to the city and county.

T. S. Eliot observed in his preface to one of the many James Joyce biographies that curiosity about the private life of a public man is useful when the subject is a man of letters, 'if the study throws light upon his published works'. James Joyce's published works would be entirely different had he not spent almost every day of his adult life with Nora Barnacle from Bowling Green in the heart of Galway city.

Two comprehensive biographies of Nora Barnacle Joyce were published during the 1980s, around the centenary of her birth, and I have relied on them without retilling the ground they have ploughed. The best by far of the many biographies of her husband is Richard Ellmann's *James Joyce* (1959).

This book was written by a Galwegian for Galwegians and for visitors or students in Galway. It is an attempt to trace the many Galway threads that run through the works of James Joyce, perhaps the most famous of Irish writers internationally.

ACKNOWLEDGEMENTS

This book grew out of a series of three articles written for the *Connacht Tribune* in January 2012 at the invitation of the editor, Dave O'Connell, who hails from Oughterard, where one of Joyce's Galway-inspired characters, Michael Furey in the short story 'The Dead', lies buried in 'the lonely churchyard on the hill'. I'm greatly indebted to Dave for giving me the opportunity to write those articles and for ongoing encouragement, friendship and good cheer. The fewer than 10,000 words in the *Connacht Tribune* articles have increased to more than 60,000 words in this book.

My greatest debt is to my former boss at RTÉ News, Ed Mulhall, who was for many years Managing Director of RTÉ News and Current Affairs, and who has always given me undying support and good counsel. He is the best editor I ever worked with and he wears his vast knowledge of the life and works of James Joyce and so many other subjects extremely lightly. His suggestions and observations have made the finished article much better than it would be otherwise.

I am also heavily indebted to Kieran Hoare, chief archivist in the James Hardiman Library at National University of Ireland Galway, and to his colleague, Marie Boran, for help and direction during repeated visits, and to Justin Furlong and his colleagues at the National Library of Ireland for similar assistance. I am especially indebted to NUI Galway for permission to publish for the first time the poem 'She Weeps Over Rahoon' in Joyce's own handwriting, with a decorative initial capital letter by his daughter Lucia, from a limited edition facsimile that Joyce presented to the university in 1935. Patria McWalter in the Galway County Archives, on Nuns' Island, also provided prompt and valuable help as did Timothy Collins, a former NUI Galway librarian and author. Tom Kenny, of Kennys Bookstore, and Ronnie O'Gorman, of the *Galway Advertiser*, answered queries readily

xiv | JOYCE COUNTY

and helpfully. I'm also very grateful to my youngest brother, Gerard, for many important suggestions on the final draft. I also owe thanks to the staff at the Dublin City Library and Archive on Pearse Street and at the British Library in London.

Two RTÉ newsroom colleagues gave me great help. Declan Dunne, Chief Sub-Editor of RTÉ Radio, cast his eagle eyes over an early draft with his usual exemplary care and Roisin Duffy translated from Italian the Joyce articles on Galway that were written over one hundred years ago in a style that is now somewhat antiquated. My current boss, Kevin Bakhurst, Managing Director of RTÉ News and Current Affairs and Deputy Director General, has been ever-helpful and generous, particularly in insisting on a work–life balance that enabled this book to be completed. So too has Michael Good, Managing Editor of RTÉ Radio News, who brought me into the newsroom when the *Irish Press* closed down in 1995.

I am indebted to Fearghal O'Boyle, Patrick O'Donoghue, Lisa Keating, Helene Pertl, Leeann Gallagher, Ellen Monnelly and Michael Brennan at Currach Press for arranging and overseeing this publication with supreme expertise and enthusiasm.

Special thanks are due to my wife, Marian, for patient endurance and perpetual encouragement.

1

WIFE

'My wife is from Galway city'

Some girl. Best thing could happen him ...
— Leopold Bloom in *Ulysses* (15:4950)

JAMES JOYCE SPENT MORE TIME IN GALWAY than anywhere else in the weeks before he embarked on permanent exile from Ireland.[1] Galway is also where he spent significant days during two of his four brief return visits to his homeland after he first sailed into exile.

Although Dublin and Dubliners dominate Joyce's writings, Galway also commands a special place because of what he saw and heard during his two visits to the city and county, and because of the Galway lore he learned from his partner and muse Nora Barnacle, who came from Bowling Green in the city centre.[2]

Joyce's principal work, *Ulysses* – which is set on 16 June 1904 to commemorate his first date with Nora Barnacle – contains several references to Galway, and his most famous short story, 'The Dead', pivots on the memory of one of Nora Barnacle's lost Galway loves. He associated that story's climactic song, 'The Lass of Aughrim', with Nora and he persuaded her mother, Annie Barnacle, to sing it for him in her home in Bowling Green during his first visit to Galway in 1909.

The heroines of *Ulysses* and 'The Dead', Molly Bloom and Gretta Conroy respectively, are heavily based on Nora Barnacle and 16 June is now widely known as Bloomsday, an annual international celebration of the fictional Molly Bloom and her husband. The character

Bertha in Joyce's only stage play, *Exiles*, is also based on Nora, as is the main female character in his last work, *Finnegans Wake*. One of his best-known poems was inspired by a visit to Galway's Rahoon Cemetery with Nora and he wrote two lengthy articles about Galway for a leading Italian newspaper during his second Galway visit in 1912. He also copied copiously from the pages of successive issues of the Galway weekly newspaper, the *Connacht Tribune*, when he was compiling the notebooks he used to compose *Finnegans Wake*.

'Everything that is noble and exalted and deep and true and moving in what I write comes, I believe, from you,' Joyce told Nora in a letter in which he heavily underlined the word 'everything'. In the same letter, written five years after they had met, he also declared: 'You are more to me than the world ... O take me into your soul of souls and then I will become indeed the poet of my race.'[3] And in another letter less than two months later, he underlined the words 'know' and 'feel' when he told her: 'I know and feel that if I am to write anything fine or noble in the future I shall do so only by listening at the doors of your heart.'[4]

An anguished cry of 'I am lost! – Nora!' changes the entire thrust and mood of *Giacomo Joyce*, the only Joyce composition that is not set in Dublin and one that he withheld from publication.[5] Similarly, a remark by the Nora-inspired character, Gretta, transforms 'The Dead' – it is a Galway woman who dramatically alters the final and linchpin story of the fifteen tales of quintessential Dubliners in the collection of that name, thereby attaching it to Galway as much as to Dublin.[6]

Joyce met Nora shortly after she had moved from Galway to Dublin, where she got work as a live-in chambermaid in Finn's Hotel near the city centre. She had been reared mostly by her maternal grandmother because of overcrowding in the family home in Bowling Green. Nora was born in the Union Workhouse (in the grounds of the current University College Hospital) in March 1884 when her parents were living on Sullivan's Lane, off Raleigh Row (the ancient road between Galway city and the Atlantic seaboard of Connemara, the northern region of which has been known for centuries as Joyce Country). She was informally fostered out to her grandmother, Catherine Healy, when her family eventually settled in No. 4, Bowling Green, the address Joyce later used in his letters from Galway. This mid-terrace house, now known as Nora Barnacle House, has one small downstairs room opening onto the street and one small upstairs room.[7]

Nora's childhood years were divided between Bowling Green and her grandmother's home in nearby Whitehall, the cul-de-sac at the east end of St Augustine Street (now the pedestrian rear entrance to the Eyre Square Shopping Centre). While living there, Nora went to school at the Convent of Mercy in Newtownsmith and she made her first communion in the pro-cathedral, midway between her grandmother's home and Bowling Green.[8] Nora left school at the age of thirteen and worked in the Presentation Convent, beside St Joseph's Church, until she left Galway.

The 1901 census lists Nora's occupation as 'laundress' and it records her living in Bowling Green with her mother, four sisters and a brother, although she was almost certainly still living in Whitehall with her grandmother and her uncle Thomas Healy at the time. Informal fostering to a relative was not uncommon in those days. One of Nora's sisters, Mary, told biographer Richard Ellmann in 1953 that Nora was sent at the age of five to a grandmother on Nuns' Island, which is directly across the River Corrib from Bowling Green.[9] This may have been Catherine Healy's address before Whitehall, or it may have been the home of Nora's paternal grandmother.

The census form also records her first name as Norah, as does her birth certificate. It was James Joyce who changed her first name by dropping the 'h' (long before he changed her last name too by marrying her). Her mother, Annie, continued to write to her as Norah for decades after she left Galway, but Joyce wrote her name as Nora (without the final 'h') from the time they met. Her initial replies to his letters were signed 'Norah Barnacle' or 'N. Barnacle', but within three months of meeting him she was signing herself 'Nora' and she continued to do so thereafter. Nora is the name of the main character in the stage play *A Doll's House*, by the Norwegian dramatist Henrik Ibsen (1828–1906), who was a major influence on the young James Joyce.

The Joyce family was not impressed with Nora at first. 'When the Joyce family met Nora Barnacle, they didn't take too well to her at all,' recalled Oughterard-born Ken Monaghan, a son of Joyce's sister May. 'Having come from a comfortable family background themselves originally, they apparently looked down on her, though they themselves were by that time living in the same straitened circumstances.'[10]

'Are "the girls" "snotty" about Nora?' Joyce asked his brother Stanislaus in a letter four months after leaving Dublin.[11] One sister, Eva, told Joyce's friend Arthur Power that she regarded Nora as 'common'.[12] And the punning observation of Joyce's father on hearing Nora's surname was as acerbic as it was funny: 'She'll never leave him.'[13]

Joyce's mother was dead for less than a year when he met Nora. He was still feeling guilty about his inability to pray at his dying mother's bedside.[14] Although his mother had found the character named Nora in *A Doll's House* 'charming', according to *Stephen Hero*, the suspicion that she may not have considered a chambermaid from Galway to be good enough for her eldest and favourite son is suggested in 'The Dead' when the Joyce character, Gabriel Conroy, recalls his own dead mother:

> A shadow passed over his face as he remembered her sullen opposition to his marriage. Some slighting phrases she had used still rankled in his memory; she had once spoken of Gretta as being country cute and this was not true of Gretta at all.

Joyce's friend Constantine Curran, a former university classmate, had no doubt but that meeting Nora changed Joyce's life. He wrote: 'For Joyce in 1904 there was no outlet but flight; whatever assistance he might give his family could be rendered from a distance, and it was fortunate for him and for us that it was in the June of this year that he met the woman whose courage and devotion confirmed his resolution to leave Dublin and saw him safely through the difficult years that lay before him.'[15]

Another long-time friend, Stuart Gilbert, said that Joyce and Nora were 'literally inseparable' from the time they met. He recalled:

> During all the years I knew him, Joyce never spent a night or even a full day away from his wife. There was the happiest understanding between them; though Nora Joyce's admiration of her husband and loyalty towards him were boundless, she had a strong personality and knew how to preserve her independence. ... Nora Joyce had what the Victorians called a fine presence and I have met few women who combined such natural dignity with as much good-heartedness and bonhomie.[16]

Joyce's first biographer, Herbert Gorman, who spent considerable time with the Joyces in Paris and whose biography was written with the cooperation of Joyce himself and two of his brothers, Stanislaus and George, described Nora as 'a miracle among women'. He wrote:

> She was neither literary-minded nor, it would seem, prepared to cope with the vagaries and temperament of an artist; yet her freshness, her humour, her joyous disposition, and her transparent honesty captivated Joyce and it was not long before he was completely in love with her. She ... reciprocated this love. With this encounter Joyce's life changed. ... Mrs Joyce was assiduous in guarding her husband from the many hangers-on and victimizers of genius who sought for anything they could get out of the writer and she transformed his home into a place where he could work in peace. If she became impatient at times before the situations that seem to her far from healthy for her husband it was but natural and a testimony to her concerns for his welfare. On the whole, her brightness of

disposition and roguish Irish humour added a delightful touch to the Joyce household.

And in the biography's acknowledgements, Gorman wrote: 'To the graciousness of Mrs James Joyce I incline an admiring head.'[17]

Arthur Power, a constant friend of the Joyces when they lived in Paris, said: 'She was a sincere and gallant woman, and his worthy companion and mate – this breath of Galway air in the intellectual hothouse of Paris.'[18] He also said that 'she was extremely shrewd; judged character in a flash, and was firm in her judgments.'[19]

Another friend from Dublin and Paris, Mary Colum, wrote:

> Nora Joyce, as I came to see as I knew her better, was not only beautiful but vivacious and humorous. Though she had but little education, she had natural aptitudes, among them a love and understanding of music. She and Joyce could be together in the realm of music, though – I later found out – she had little comprehension of literature, and none at all of the sort of literature Joyce produced.

She added: 'James Joyce was markedly devoted to Nora; her personality was full of interest to him, and he delighted in her sayings and snappy remarks.'[20]

Mary Colum's husband, the poet and writer Padraic Colum, concurred. 'Mrs Joyce, with her rich personality, her sincere and steadfast character, is an ideal companion for a man who has to do Joyce's work,' he wrote. 'She talks about Galway to me, and the old rain-soaked town comes before me as she talks about [Eyre] Square, the churches, the convent in which were passed many of her years.' He added: 'Mrs Joyce gives us the best tea and the nicest cakes that are to be had in any house in Paris.'[21] Another visitor from Dublin, Kenneth Reddin, recalled: 'I remember ... Mrs Joyce's beautiful Galway voice, her hospitality and constant good humour.'[22]

A French journalist and writer who became a family friend, Nino

Frank, described another 1920s Paris party thus: 'There I saw Mrs Joyce, a beauty faithful to her portrait, barely powdered by the years, patient, gentle, and infinitely distant, the only one of the household who occasionally made use of English.'[23]

And Joyce's brother Stanislaus, who was displaced by Nora as the writer's chief confidante, said of James: 'Up until the time of his death ... he was apart from her only for a very few weeks, and then unwillingly.'[24]

Joyce was only twenty-two years old when he met Nora and she was barely out of her teens.[25] The Joyce character in *Ulysses*, Stephen Dedalus, is also aged twenty-two. When he tries to mumble some poetry while lying on the ground, semi-conscious from drunkenness and a blow to the face, his temporary guardian, Leopold Bloom, observes: 'A girl. Some girl. Best thing could happen him ...'[26]

When Joyce met Nora he had moved away from his family home and was living in a furnished room at No. 60 Shelbourne Road (on the main walking route between Dublin city centre and the football stadium on Lansdowne Road). The meeting point for their first date was outside No. 1 Merrion Square, a building at the corner of Merrion Square North and Merrion Street Lower that is visible from the front door of Nora's workplace, Finn's Hotel, and that was the former family home of Sir William Wilde, author of *Lough Corrib, Its Shores and Islands,* and father of Oscar Wilde.[27] Nora was unable to keep their initial appointment, and when they first walked out together on 16 June Joyce was staying temporarily with friends in nearby Sandymount because he had not paid his rent for No. 60 Shelbourne Road.[28]

Joyce began writing poetry for and about Nora shortly after they met and a handful of these poems are included in his first collection and first published book, *Chamber Music.* Nora later told him that she found the poems 'enchanting' and he replied that 'the beauty of your soul outshone that of my verses'. He added: 'There was something in you higher than anything I had put into them. And so for this reason the book of verses is for you. It holds the desire of my youth and you, darling, were the fulfilment of that desire.'[29]

Nora eloped with Joyce four months after they met and they lived together for the rest of their lives in Italy, Switzerland, France, England and the part of the Austro-Hungarian empire that is now Croatia.[30] Despite Joyce's initial fears that Nora was 'one of those plants which cannot be safely transplanted',[31] she returned to Galway only twice, for short holidays in 1912 and 1922.[32]

Joyce cast Nora in a Galway play, the Aran Island based classic *Riders to the Sea* by John Millington Synge, that was the centrepiece of a season of plays that he staged in Zurich in 1918 when he and other expatriates were sheltering from World War I in neutral Switzerland.

Nora played the role of Cathleen – 'a girl of about twenty' – and Joyce urged the other actors to try to copy her strong Galway accent and West of Ireland speech rhythms. He said that Nora 'was born within sight of Aran'. Although he had never warmed to Synge personally, he wrote in the programme notes: 'Synge's first play, written in Paris in 1902 out of his memories of Aran ... the ear and the heart mislead one gravely if this brief scene is not the work of a tragic poet.'[33]

The Aran Islands are among the places that Joyce toured during his 1912 Galway visit, his last time in Ireland and the only Irish holiday he had with Nora and their children. During the visit he wrote two lengthy feature articles about the Aran Islands and Galway city for the main Trieste newspaper, *Il Piccolo della Sera*, whose editor was learning English from him. He also sent a postcard with a picture of an aged Claddagh fisherman to a friend in Trieste.[34] On the back of it he wrote one sentence: 'A portrait of the artist as an old man' with the word 'old' underlined. He signed the card 'Stephen Dedalus' (after the hero of *Stephen Hero* and *A Portrait of the Artist as a Young Man*). The postcard, from the Valentine colour series, shows a Claddagh fisherman with a very weather-beaten face sitting on a stone bollard on Nimmo's Pier or the Claddagh Basin. The caption says: 'The oldest Claddagh fisherman, Galway.' The card is date-stamped Galway, 11.15 p.m., 26 July 1912. A copy is on display in the Joyce Museum in Trieste.

The Joyce family stayed in Michael Healy's house on Dominic Street for four weeks between mid-July and mid-August 1912. During that time Joyce sailed to the Aran Islands, cycled to Oughterard, took a train to Clifden, went rowing on the Corrib and attended the Galway Races. 'Nora's uncle feeds us in great style and I row and cycle and drive a good deal,' Joyce wrote to his brother Stanislaus from No. 4 Bowling Green on 7 August, the day of that year's Galway Plate.

Eighteen horses competed for the Galway Plate and the race was won by Noble Grecian, a portent, perhaps, for the man who was planning to write his own epic novel based on the tale of the noble and ancient Greek hero Odysseus (Ulysses in Latin) and who would insist that the book's cover must match precisely the blue of the Greek national flag. But Joyce did not enjoy his day at the Galway Races, although, according to that week's *Connacht Tribune*, 'it is doubtful if a better day's racing was ever provided for patrons at Ballybrit than was witnessed on Wednesday'. The newspaper added that 'there was only one brief shower during the afternoon ... which in no way marred the pleasure of the crowd'. However, Joyce complained to Nora two weeks later: 'I told you of my grief at Galway Races. I feel it still.'[35]

Joyce was unhappy and frustrated in the summer of 1912 because he was still very much a struggling writer. His thirtieth birthday had passed and most of his former college friends had established themselves in professional careers. More than six years had gone by since he completed *Dubliners* and the semi-autobiographical *Stephen Hero*, but he had been unable to find a publisher for either work and he was rewriting *Stephen Hero* as *A Portrait of the Artist as a Young Man*. His only substantial published work at that time comprised a handful of short stories in the small-circulation magazine *Irish Homestead*, sundry newspaper articles, and the poetry collection *Chamber Music*, which had sold fewer than 200 copies in the five years since it was published in 1907.[36]

The short story collection, *Dubliners*, anchored by 'The Dead' and described by Joyce as 'my nicely polished looking glass' for the Irish people, was still no nearer publication in summer 1912, several years after he had signed contracts with prominent London and Dublin publishing houses.[37] His letter to Nora two weeks after the Galway

Plate followed another fruitless meeting in Dublin with the publisher, who had added new, insurmountable obstacles and effectively repudiated the contract.

'I am like a man walking in his sleep,' he wrote to her from Dublin while she remained in Galway with their children, Giorgio and Lucia. He said he sat in despair in the publisher's office 'thinking of the book I have written, the child which I have carried for years and years in the womb of the imagination as you carried in your womb the children you love, and of how I had fed it day after day out of my brain and my memory'. He added: 'I hope that the day may come when I shall be able to give you the fame of being beside me when I have entered into my Kingdom.'[38]

Fame was still a decade away, but the final visit to Galway and Dublin sparked Joyce's most creative and productive years. On his hejira to mainland Europe by boat and rail he wrote on the back of his worthless publishing contract the searing poem 'Gas from a Burner' in which he ridiculed his reneging publisher. He then began work on *Ulysses*, *Exiles* and most of *Pomes Penyeach* shortly after returning to Trieste and permanent exile.[39]

The visits to Oughterard and Clifden were the closest he got to his ancestral Joyce Country in Connemara. In Oughterard he was amused to find a headstone in the cemetery inscribed 'J. Joyce' and in Clifden he failed to find the Italian inventor and engineer Guglielmo Marconi, who had established the world's first wireless telegraphy station there in 1907 and who he hoped to interview for *Il Piccolo della Sera*. He tried to get a free train ticket from Dublin to Galway in 1909 by presenting a card to the railway company manager saying he was writing a series of articles on Ireland for the Italian paper.[40] But the Clifden trip was not in vain. Joyce has preserved the memory of the now long-gone Marconi Station in *Finnegans Wake* as 'the loftly marconimasts from Clifden'.[41]

Throughout his exile, Joyce carried with him from country to country and from apartment to apartment the Joyce family coat of arms, a testament to his enduring pride in his ancient Connemara ancestry. Although his father and grandfather were from a Cork branch of the Connemara clan, he was proud to bear the name of one of the Tribes of Galway and to be living with a Galway woman. 'The family comes, of course, from the west of Ireland (Joyce's country) but mine is a southern offshoot of the tribe.[42] My wife is from Galway city,' he wrote to a London literary agent.[43] He also noted in the first of his *Il Piccolo* articles that a well-known seventeenth-century decorative map of Galway city 'was the work of Henry Joyce'. And he wrote at length in that newspaper about the infamous murders in Maamtrasna in Joyce Country in Connemara in 1882 – the year of his birth – in which all five victims and some of the accused were Joyces and which resulted in a public hanging in Galway jail, beside Nuns' Island (see Chapter 3).

Another Galway city public hanging, though from an earlier century and possibly apocryphal, was retailed colourfully by Joyce in *Il Piccolo*. It may also have prompted him to name a disreputable character who appears in *Ulysses*, *A Portrait of the Artist as a Young Man* and *Stephen Hero* after the fifteenth-century Mayor of Galway and chief magistrate, James Lynch, who reputedly ordered that his own convict son be hanged and who is said to have carried out the execution himself at the family's front window. The Lynch Window is now relocated to Market Street, where it is visible from the front door of the Barnacle house in Bowling Green and Joyce asked about it during his Galway visits (See Chapter 3).

Exile took Joyce and Nora back to Trieste and subsequently to Zurich (twice), Paris and London. They moved to London for several months during 1931 in order to establish residency so as to be able to marry formally after they had been living together as husband and wife for twenty-seven years.[44] Although Joyce had written to his brother Stanislaus in May 1905, 'Why should I have brought Nora to a priest or a lawyer to make her swear away her life to me?' he later claimed that they had gone through a form of marriage ceremony in 1904 at the start of their exile and he considered them to be married 'by habit and repute'.[45] He regularly referred to Nora as 'my wife', 'my bride' or 'my little Galway bride'.[46] However, legal advice on the children's inheritance rights led to a hastily arranged marriage ceremony at a London register office on 4 July 1931 – an event that attracted international media attention.[47]

Joyce tried to keep the wedding plan secret but newspapermen laid siege to the register office and to his London address.[48] 'All day the bell went and the telephone. Even at midnight when we came back from supper there was a reporter posted on the steps,' Joyce told his son Giorgio.[49] He explained to Giorgio that the 1904 Austrian wedding was invalid and that it was necessary to marry under English law for 'testamentary reasons'. He added: 'Try to look as natural as possible so that people meeting you may not perceive that you have been turned into honest citizens all of a sudden.'[50]

The wedding lunch was held in the home, in Hampstead, of the Belfast-born journalist and essayist Robert Lynd, the author of the evocative 1912 essay 'Galway of the Races' (and the man who persuaded the artist Paul Henry to go to Achill Island, where he remained for seven years and began painting the landscapes that would make him famous). At a follow-up party in the same house a few nights later, Joyce sang 'Phil the Fluther's Ball' and 'Shule Aroon' and recited his own 'Anna Livia Plurabelle' (in a rendition that one guest, the book publisher, Victor Gollancz, deemed 'lovely beyond description').[51]

International newspaper coverage of the wedding dismayed and bewildered the Joyces, however, and it also greatly embarrassed the Barnacle family in Galway. The news 'caused utter consternation in Galway, particularly among neighbours of the Barnacle family in Bowling Green', according to Nora's Galway biographer Padraic O Laoi. 'Tongues wagged in that close community and the neighbours placed more store in the newspaper story than they did in the explanation offered by the Barnacles,' he wrote.[52]

Despite the embarrassment, Joyce maintained regular contact with his Galway in-laws (as they now literally were). Nora's sister Kathleen travelled to London for a long holiday there with James and Nora. Joyce continued to correspond with Nora's mother, Annie, who also occasionally sent him articles from the Galway newspapers. He also asked his main patroness, Harriet Weaver, to send a copy of the newly published first biography of him to Mrs Barnacle at No. 4, Bowling Green, adding: 'It will give her great pleasure to have it.'[53]

Annie's brother, Michael Healy, also appears to have been unperturbed by the twenty-seven-year delay that preceded the formal marriage, even though he was a staunch Catholic and a member of the Men's Sodality in the Jesuit Church on Sea Road. 'Half the clergy in the city were at his funeral,' Joyce noted after Michael Healy died suddenly in 1936 while attending Mass in the Jesuit Church. Joyce told his former university classmate Constantine Curran that Michael Healy was 'the only friend I had in Ireland except yourself', adding: 'He had been a staunch and loyal friend of mine for 25 years and I miss him very much. He would have walked round Ireland to do me any service.'[54]

Michael Healy was the Barnacle family member to whom Joyce was closest. As well as accommodating Joyce and Nora and their children in his home at No. 18 Dominic Street during their 1912 visit to Galway, he corresponded regularly with them – almost every month during 1915 – and he sent them money via a circuitous route when they were short during World War I. He bought boots for Nora when she was young (at a time when many Galway city children went barefoot) and he tried to find Lucia when she was on holiday in Ireland and out of contact with her parents. Joyce told his aunt Josephine that Michael Healy was 'one of the very few wellwishers I have in [Ireland] and would do a great deal to help me as he has often done'.[55] Michael Healy also kept in contact with Joyce's ailing father, John Stanislaus Joyce, in Dublin. In one of his last letters to his son, John Stanislaus wrote in 1931 (the year of his death): 'I often hear from Mr Healy, whose generous gifts I should be glad if you would also acknowledge.'[56]

Joyce addressed Michael Healy as 'My dear Mr Healy' and he sent him first editions of all of his books. For Christmas 1933 he sent him a case of thirteen-year-old red wine from Avignon, explaining that Chateauneuf du Pape had originally been known as Vin de S. Patrice after Saint Patrick.

Michael Healy rose to the position of Her Majesty's Inspector of Custom and Excise and also Receiver of Wrecks in Galway, based at No. 26 Dominic Street.[57] He was transferred to Dublin for a time and returned to Galway to live on the Crescent (or Palmyra Crescent as it is recorded in the 1911 census) and at No. 16 St Mary's Terrace, a late-nineteenth-century development just off Nile Lodge at the bottom of Taylor's Hill.

Michael Healy's death severed Joyce's last regular link with Galway. His last recorded contact with the Barnacles was in the summer of 1940 when he and Nora and their son and grandson had to flee Paris after the German invasion of France. He sent a postcard dated 18 June 1940 to Annie Barnacle in Bowling Green addressing her as 'Dear Mrs Barnacle'. He wrote: 'This is our new address. We, Nora, Giorgio, Stevie and I are well. Lucia is still down at la Baule with her doctor and well also. We hope you all are too.' (For details of Lucia's illness, see Chapter 8.)

Annie Barnacle died five months later, however, aged eighty-two, and the news of her death made Joyce cry like a baby, according to his grandson Stephen.[58] Joyce and Nora were the chief beneficiaries of Annie's will – Joyce had told Constantine Curran in 1936 that she 'has always been a kind of worshipper of mine' (see Chapter 8). His emotionalism when she died would have been heightened by mounting worries about the unfolding world war and the unfavourable critical and public reaction to his last work, *Finnegans Wake*, which he had been writing for the previous seventeen years. Of even greater concern was his own poor health and Nora's, and particularly the fate of Lucia, whom he would be forced to leave behind in hospital in occupied France a few weeks later when the rest of the family managed to gain entry to neutral Switzerland in mid-December 1940.

Lucia had been diagnosed with schizophrenia in the early 1930s and she was confined to hospital more and more. 'Joyce spared no pains and spent large sums in attempts to have his daughter cured, but unavailingly, and the last years of his life were clouded by this grief,' recalled his friend Stuart Gilbert.[59] Those years, wrote Richard

Ellmann, 'were pervaded by a frantic and unhappily futile effort to cure her by every means known to medicine as well as by simples of his own devising'.[60] In a letter to a friend in 1935 Joyce wrote: 'There are moments and hours when I have nothing in my heart but rage and despair, a blind man's rage and despair.'[61]

Joyce outlived Annie Barnacle by just over two months. His return to Zurich lasted less than a month. One of his last letters was to the Mayor of Zurich to thank him for helping to secure the entry permits: 'The connection between me and your hospitable city extends over a period of nearly 40 years and in these painful times I feel highly honoured that I should owe my presence here in large part to the personal guaranty of Zurich's first citizen,' he wrote five days before Christmas.[62]

Five days earlier Joyce had interrupted his family's rail journey to Zurich at Geneva to meet the former Irish diplomat Seán Lester, who was now acting secretary general of the League of Nations and whose help he had sought in trying to secure an exit visa from occupied France for Lucia. Nora told Lester that she had been trying in recent years to induce Joyce to return to Ireland, but Joyce said 'he felt it would not be very dignified to go home in the present circumstances'.[63]

Ten days into the new year, Joyce was taken by ambulance to a Zurich hospital. 'A feverish delirium set in, and with increasing urgency he repeated the same command – that Nora Joyce, who was sitting beside him, should set up her bed next to his,' recalled Zurich-based family friend Carola Giedion-Weckler.[64] But the doctors sent Nora home when his condition stabilised. Before she could return, however, he died in the early hours of Monday, 13 January 1941, of a neglected, perforated ulcer.

2

GRETTA

'I'd love to see Galway again'

Rain on Rahoon falls softly, softly falling.
— From *She Weeps Over Rahoon*

I gave up everything for him, religion, family, my own peace.
— Bertha in *Exiles*, Third Act

She was just a young thin pale soft shy slim slip of a thing, sauntering.
— From 'Anna Livia Plurabelle', *Finnegans Wake*

'I'D LOVE TO SEE GALWAY AGAIN,' pleads the Nora Barnacle character, Gretta Conroy, in one of several references to her home place in 'The Dead'. Mentions of Nuns' Island and Aughrim trigger Gretta's emotional recollections in between symbolic references to the Aran Islands and Oughterard in the short story that has been acclaimed as the best in the English language.

Joyce confirmed to Nora that he based the character Gretta Conroy on her. 'Do you remember', he asked her in a letter, 'the three adjectives I have used in "The Dead" in speaking of your body. They are these: "musical and strange and perfumed".'[1] Elsewhere in 'The Dead', Gretta's husband, Gabriel, recalls writing to her that 'there is no word tender enough to be your name', repeating almost identically the words that Joyce had written to Nora early in their relationship.[2]

Joyce also told Nora that the song that transfixes Gretta and transforms the story, 'The Lass of Aughrim', is 'your song'. In a letter written on the kitchen table of the Bowling Green house in 1909, three years after he had finished 'The Dead', Joyce told Nora: 'I was singing an hour ago your song *The Lass of Aughrim*. The tears come into my eyes and my voice trembles with emotion when I sing that lovely air. It was worth coming to Ireland to have got it from your poor kind mother.'[3] In another letter to Nora from Bowling Green five days earlier, he had written that Annie Barnacle 'sang for me *The Lass of Aughrim* but she does not like to sing me the last verses in which the lovers exchange their tokens'.[4]

The fictional Michael Furey in 'The Dead' is based on Michael 'Sonny' Bodkin, who died tragically young while courting Nora in 1900. He is buried in Rahoon Cemetery.[5] Joyce has recalled that Nora told him she had 'many love-affairs' before she left Galway, including 'one when quite young with a boy who died'. He said she told him she was 'laid up at news of his death'.[6] In 'The Dead', Joyce wrote that Gretta 'had locked in her heart for so many years that image of her lover's eyes when he had told her that he did not wish to live'. And the eyes of the story's Joyce character, Gabriel Conroy, filled with 'generous tears' when he recalled Gretta's description of her final meeting with her lover in the back garden in Nuns' Island and 'he imagined he saw the form of a young man standing under a dripping tree'.

'Sonny' Bodkin died of tuberculosis at the age of nineteen and the last words spoken by anyone in 'The Dead' are Gretta's anguished cries when she recalls hearing of the death of her young Galway lover. These words – 'O, the day that I heard that, that he was dead!' – reverberate in one of the few public utterances of Nora Barnacle that have been recorded by her friends. Discussing first love one evening in Paris she remarked: 'There's nothing like it. I remember when I was a girl and a young man fell in love with me, and he came and sang in the rain under an apple-tree outside my windows, and he caught tuberculosis and died.'[7]

Michael 'Sonny' Bodkin lived at No. 1 Prospect Hill (now Richardson's pub on the corner of Eyre Square and Prospect Hill) where the 1901 census records his parents, Patrick and Winifred Bodkin, both native Galwegians, running a provisions shop.

In 'The Dead', which Joyce completed four years after he met Nora but before he visited Galway, the cemetery where the 'dark lover lies' is in Oughterard (where Nora's errant father, Thomas Barnacle, often worked as a journeyman baker). Joyce cycled to Oughterard Cemetery during his 1912 Galway visit and he found it 'exactly as I imagined it' when writing 'The Dead'. He was also amused to find one of the headstones was to 'J. Joyce'.[8]

Galway is also the destination of the 'journey westward' that Gretta's husband, Gabriel Conroy, must make at the end of 'The Dead', whether physically or in dreams in the sleep into which he was falling. The journey westward begins in the story's final paragraph, which contains strong echoes of the only poem Joyce wrote about Galway and Nora Barnacle, 'She Weeps Over Rahoon'. 'The Dead' ends in Oughterard with snow 'falling softly' and 'softly falling ... upon every part of the lonely churchyard on the hill where Michael Furey lay buried' and the opening line of the poem 'She Weeps Over Rahoon' begins with the words 'Rain on Rahoon falls softly, softly falling'.

In the poem, which Joyce wrote in Trieste shortly after his 1912 visit to Galway, Nora Barnacle is imagined standing beside him in Rahoon Cemetery mourning at Michael Bodkin's grave. The poem was not published until 1927 when Joyce released the autobiographical collection *Pomes Penyeach* in Paris. He sent a copy of a special limited edition of the collection, with what he called 'extremely beautiful' decorative lettering designed and illustrated by his daughter Lucia, to the library of University College Galway, as it was then known, in 1935.

In a handwritten covering letter to the college librarian John Howley he said that the national libraries in London and Paris already had copies and he added:

I wished to offer a copy to your library not only because the designer of the lettrines is a grand-daughter of your city and the writer of these verses bears one of its tribal names, but also as a small acknowledgement of a great debt of gratitude to Mr [Michael] Healy himself for his kindness and courtesy during so many years.[9]

Joyce conceived the special edition of *Pomes Penyeach* to try to boost Lucia's artistic confidence, after she had abandoned a promising career as a professional dancer and had begun to exhibit signs of ill health. He copied in his own handwriting the thirteen poems in the collection (which he had published initially to reassure friends who were worried about the impenetrability of his ongoing *Work in Progress* that he could still write simple English) and had a limited edition of twenty-five facsimiles printed on rare Japanese vellum, with the initial letter of each poem elaborately illustrated by Lucia. The NUIG copy is marked Number 12 of 25.[10]

The limited edition was published in Paris in 1932 by the Obelisk Press, bound in green silk with gilt lettering. On the title page Joyce wrote: 'Initial letters designed and illuminated by Lucia Joyce' and on the tailpiece he added, again in his own handwriting: 'This edition limited to 25 copies numbered 1–25 and signed by James Joyce.' The book's publication price was 1,000 francs a copy (about 15 pounds sterling) and Joyce told Michael Healy that 'it ought to be worth much more as years go by for there are only 25 copies in existence and the mould has been destroyed'.

Joyce explained to Lucia in a letter written in Italian (the usual language of their correspondence):

After the departure of Mama's uncle [Michael Healy] from Dublin I wanted to make him a present. Knowing he would never accept money I bought one of the last copies of *Pomes Penyeach* still extant and I presented it in our name (that is,

yours and mine) to the library of the University of Galway
(biblioteca dell'Universita di Galway), as you are a grandchild
of that ancient city and I am a descendant of one of its tribes.
They had a special reading desk made and the beautiful book is
now on exhibit in the centre of the Library. The librarian, Professor Howley, came to Paris during our absence here, as you
can see from the enclosed visiting card, to thank me (and you)
'for the exquisite gift'.[11]

The gift is still in the possession of the university (now NUIG)
and it is kept with other rare manuscripts in the Special Collections
room in the James Hardiman Library. The edition shows that Joyce's
own handwritten version of 'She Weeps Over Rahoon' differs slightly
from most published versions of the poem through the addition of a
dash between the verses and of another comma and an exclamation
mark in the second verse.[12]

A second poem in the *Pomes Penyeach* collection also carries
Galway echoes and was also written shortly after the 1912 visit. Joyce
wrote 'Watching the Needleboats at San Sabba' while observing his
brother Stanislaus compete in a sculling race near Trieste and recalling the boats of the Galway rowing clubs that he had seen on the
Corrib the previous summer. He had arrived in Galway on the eve of
the annual regatta and he would have walked or taken an excursion
boat to Menlo with Nora.[13]

Joyce also sent one of the Paris 1932 limited editions containing
'She Weeps Over Rahoon' to Annie Barnacle in Bowling Green, saying
he hoped she would be glad to have it 'as a proof of your granddaugh-
ter's delicate talent'.[14]

Rahoon Cemetery and 'Sonny' Bodkin are also mentioned in the
notes Joyce wrote for his only stage play *Exiles*. This three-act play is
set in the 'Summer of the year 1912' – the summer of Joyce's last visit
to Ireland and the only time he and Nora were on holidays together in
Ireland – and he started to write notes for it in the year after that visit.

These notes – in Joyce's own handwriting and now preserved in the State University of New York, Buffalo – show how much he retained and recycled from his visit to Rahoon Cemetery and from what Nora had told him about her Galway childhood. They contain several references to Galway and Rahoon and to Nora's early years and friends.

In a note dated 12 November 1913, on the Nora character, Bertha, he wrote 'convent garden (Galway)' and he referred to Michael Bodkin and a bracelet he had given to Nora as well as to the cream sweets that her next Galway boyfriend, Willie Mulvagh, gave her.

In another note on Nora/Bertha, written the next day, he wrote:

Graveyard at Rahoon by moonlight where Bodkin's grave is. He lies in the grave. She sees his tomb (family vault) and weeps ... He is dark, unrisen, killed by love and life, young. The earth holds him. Bodkin died. Kearns died. In the convent they called her the man-killer ... Rahoon her people. She weeps over Rahoon too, over him whom her love has killed, the dark boy whom, as the earth, she embraces in death and disintegration. He is her buried life, her past. His attendant images are the trinkets and toys of girlhood (bracelet, cream sweets, pale-green lily of the valley, the convent garden). His symbols are music and the sea, liquid formless earth in which are buried the drowned soul and body. There are tears of commiseration. She is Magdalen who weeps remembering the loves she could not return.

An equally detailed note for the play was created out of what Nora told Joyce about another one of her lost Galway childhood friends, Emily Lyons, with whom she played in her grandmother's garden. Emily lived on Abbeygate Street, which adjoins Whitehall, where Nora was living with her grandmother, and the two schoolgirl pals played together up to the day before Emily emigrated to Boston in 1895, leaving Nora forlorn.

This note begins with a happy recollection:

It is Christmas in Galway, a moonlit Christmas eve with snow. She is carrying picture almanacs to her grandmother's house to be ornamented with holly and ivy. The evenings are spent in the house of a friend where they give her lemonade. Lemonade and currantcake are also her grandmother's Christmas fare for her. She thumps the piano and sits with her dark-complexioned gipsy-looking girlfriend Emily Lyons on the windowsill.

Nora was aged only eleven years when Emily emigrated and their parting presaged Nora's loss of three boyfriends during her teenage Galway years. The note goes on:

It is the quay of Galway harbour on a bright morning. The emigrant ship is going away and Emily, her dark friend, stands on deck going out to America. They kiss and cry bitterly. But she believes that some day her friend will come back as she promises. She cries for the pain of separation and for the dangers of the sea that threaten the girl who is going away. The girl is older than she and has no lover. She too has no lover. Her sadness is brief. She is alone, friendless, in her grandmother's garden and can see the garden, lonely now, in which the day before she played with her friend. Her grandmother consoles her, gives her a clean new pinafore to wear and buttoned boots, a present from her uncle, and nice bread and butter to eat and a big fire to sit down to.

The notes continue to draw on Nora's recollections of her Galway youth:

The boots suggest their giver, her uncle and she feels vaguely the forgotten cares and affections among [which] she grew up. She thinks of them kindly, not because they were kind to *her* but because they were kind to her girlself which is now gone and because they are part of it, hidden away even from herself in her memory. The note of regret is ever present and finds utterance at last in the tears which fill her eyes as she sees her friend go. A departure. A friend, her own youth, going away. A faint glimmer of lesbianism irradiates this mind. This girl too is dark, even like a gipsy, and she too, like the dark lover who sleeps in Rahoon, is going away from her, the man-killer and perhaps also the lover-killer, over the dark sea which is distance, the extinction of interest and death. They have no male lovers and are moved vaguely one towards the other. The friend is older, stronger, can travel alone, braver, a prophecy of a later dark male.

Emily Lyons has also been identified as the model for a *Ulysses* character, Hester Stanhope, a Gibraltar childhood friend of Molly Bloom, who she recalls in her soliloquy (see Chapter 4). The passenger manifest of the steamship *Peruvian* which sailed from Galway to Boston on 24 August 1895 includes an Emily D. Lyons, aged fourteen, from Abbeygate Street, Galway.[15] If Emily did keep her promise to Nora to return to Galway some day, she almost certainly did not do so until after 1904 when Nora had moved away. Nora herself returned to Galway only twice after she left in 1904, for short holidays in 1912 and 1922.

Joyce's notes for *Exiles*, published in 1951, the year Nora died, confirm that the play, like 'The Dead' and 'She Weeps Over Rahoon' before it and like much of *Ulysses* after it, draws heavily on his obsession with Nora's former and potential lovers. An added autobiographical leitmotiv was Joyce's horror and fascination at how Nora's beauty continued to attract admirers, coupled with his own difficulties with monogamy during the first decade and a half of his life with Nora.[16]

The Nora character in *Exiles*, Bertha, is the wife of Richard Rowan, 'a writer'. She is 'a young woman of graceful build', who has 'dark grey eyes, patient in expression, and soft features'. Her manner is 'cordial and self-possessed'. During a return visit to Dublin with her husband, Bertha is being importuned by his former close friend, Robert Hand, a successful journalist.

Emotionally charged recriminations abound in the play, which Joyce began to prepare after his bitter final departure from Ireland in 1912 and which is more autobiographical and candidly transparent about his life with Nora than any of his other works.[17] 'You told me I was hanging a weight about my neck,' Richard reminds Robert in an obvious reference to the gibes of Joyce's friends when he eloped with Nora in 1904. 'Everyone knows that you ran away with a young girl,' Robert replies. 'How shall I put it? With a young girl not exactly your equal.'

Bertha, too, voices what might be blunt truths about Nora's tough early years of exile with Joyce and about the gossip and gibes in Galway and Dublin over their unmarried status. 'I gave up everything for him,' she says, 'religion, family, my own peace.' She adds: 'I am only a thing he got entangled with and my son is – the nice name they give those children. Do you think I am a stone? Do you think I don't see it in their eyes and in their manner when they have to meet me?'

This outburst comes in a conversation with Beatrice, a young woman with whom Richard has been flirting in correspondence and in person. The conversation goes on:

BEATRICE: Do not let them humble you, Mrs Rowan.
BERTHA (*haughtily*): Humble me! I am very proud of myself, if you want to know. What have they ever done for him? I made him a man. What are they all in his life? No more than the dirt under his boots! (*She stands up and walks excitedly to and fro*) He can despise me, too, like the rest of them – now. And you can despise me. But you will never humble me, any of you.

Bertha also reminds Richard of her lonely nights of exile, similar to Nora's when Joyce was absorbed in his work or out carousing:

BERTHA: I used to sit there, waiting, with the poor child with his toys, waiting till he got sleepy ... I was so sad. I was alone, Dick, forgotten by you and by all. I felt my life was ended ... I used to think of Ireland and about ourselves.

RICHARD: Ourselves?

BERTHA: Yes. Ourselves. Not a day passes that I do not see ourselves, you and me, as we were when we met first. Every day of my life I see that. Was I not true to you all that time?

RICHARD (*sighs deeply*): Yes, Bertha. You were my bride in exile.

BERTHA: Wherever you go, I will follow you. If you wish to go away now I will go with you.

A number of other strongly autobiographical references litter the play. Richard, like Gabriel Conroy in 'The Dead' and Stephen Dedalus in *Ulysses*, is reminded several times of his mother's death and his poor relationship with her before she died. Bertha accuses him of making her unhappy 'as you made your dead mother unhappy and killed her'. Then, reversing the nickname Nora had been given in Galway, she adds: 'Woman-killer. That is your name.'

Elsewhere, Robert tells Richard that he has given Bertha 'a new and rich life' and that he has 'made her all that she is. A strange and wonderful personality'. But Richard replies: 'Is it worth what I have taken from her – her girlhood, her laughter, her young beauty, the hopes of her young heart?'

Early in the play Robert tells Bertha, 'Your face is a flower too – but more beautiful. A wild flower blowing in a hedge,' words that are almost identical to the words Joyce used to describe Nora in many letters to her, and to his description of Molly Bloom in *Ulysses*.[18]

A phrase an admirer had used to Nora in Trieste – 'the sun shines out of your face' – is recycled by the Rowans' housekeeper to Bertha, and the housekeeper's further attempt to reassure Bertha suggests how Nora's mother Annie might have described Joyce's behaviour in her kitchen in Bowling Green in 1909. 'Yes,' she says, 'I can see him sitting on the kitchen table, swinging his legs and spinning out of him yards of talk about you and him and Ireland and all kinds of devilment.'

And Bertha's observation that 'I do not understand anything that he writes ... I don't even understand half of what he says to me sometimes!' supports the belief that Nora read little of Joyce's works and his own claim that 'men of great genius' were 'not attracted by cultivated and refined women', but 'preferred simple women with sensual and nebulous minds' or else 'wanted the soul of his loved one to be entirely a slow and painstaking creation of his own'.[19]

Also in *Exiles*, Richard mentions 'a book of sketches', which is a probable reference to *Giacomo Joyce*, the prose poem notes that Joyce wrote in Trieste but that were not published until after his death, which contain the lines: 'I am lost! – Nora!'

Joyce's description of Bertha is not unlike a glimpse he gives of another Nora-inspired heroine, Anna Livia Plurabelle in *Finnegans Wake*.[20] Bertha, after nearly eight years of difficult exile and 'marriage', is still 'a young woman of graceful build' and 'soft features' with a 'cordial and self-possessed manner' in 1912. But the depiction of Anna Livia Plurabelle suggests it is Joyce's own recollection of his first sighting of Nora Barnacle as she walked along Nassau Street eight years earlier, in June 1904, shortly after her arrival from Galway. 'She was just a young thin pale soft shy slim slip of a thing, sauntering,' he wrote.[21]

Finnegans Wake may also contain a partial account of Joyce and Nora's first date, if Nora is 'the redheaded girl' and if 'my farfather out at the west' refers to Joyce's forefathers in Joyce Country in Connemara, and if, further, 'that brewer' is another of Nora's former Galway lovers, Willie Mulvagh, who worked in Joe Young's mineral water plant on Eglinton Street. The passage is:

> It was when I was in my farfather out at the west and she and myself, the redheaded girl, firstnighting down Sycamore Lane. Fine feelplay we had of it mid the kissabets frisking in the kool kurkle dusk of the lushiness. My perfume of the pampas, say she (meaning me) putting out her netherlights, and I'd sooner one precious sip at your pure mountain dew than enrich my acquaintance with that big brewer's belch.[22]

'Butterman's Lane' in *Finnegans Wake* is a likely corruption of Buttermilk Lane, the shortest route between Nora's childhood homes in Bowling Green and Whitehall.[23]

Nora's Galway childhood memories are also likely to have motivated Joyce to include two barely disguised Galway priests in his books. She told him shortly after they met how a Catholic curate from St Joseph's Church on Presentation Road had tried to abuse her when she was aged sixteen and working in the Presentation Convent. Joyce weaved the name of a Galway priest into the manuscript he was writing when he met her, the incomplete autobiographical novel *Stephen Hero*, which he later condensed greatly and refashioned as *A Portrait of the Artist as a Young Man*.

In *Stephen Hero*, Father Moran is the name of a young priest who infuriates the hero, Stephen Dedalus (based on the young Joyce), by lingering too long after weekly Gaelic League Irish language classes to chat with the young woman Stephen is besotted with and whose presence at the classes is the only reason Stephen attends them.

'Father Moran', who 'had a neat head of curly black hair and expressive black eyes' and who 'was for many reasons a great favourite with the ladies', was based, according to the Joyce biographer Peter Costello, on a curate in the parish of Rahoon, Fr John Moran, who had made inappropriate advances on the young Nora Barnacle when she was working at the Presentation Convent.[24] Joyce told his brother Stanislaus that Nora told him that the priest who tried to abuse her was 'a nice young man with black curly hairs on his head'.[25]

Nora also told Joyce that Father Moran, who was originally from near Tuam, had told her to say in confession that it was a man, not a priest, who had touched her. Joyce repeated her account to his brother Stanislaus and he also referred to it in a letter to Nora in 1912, when he asked her: 'Can ... the priesteen write my verses?'[26]

In *Stephen Hero* Joyce also wrote that Father Moran 'smiled and looked archly at Stephen' when Stephen told him that their mutual girlfriend had praised his tenor voice. And he gave to Father Moran the words: 'One must not believe all the complimentary things the ladies say of us ... The ladies are a little given to – what shall I say – fibbing, I am afraid.'

Father Moran also seems to be Joyce's target in *Finnegans Wake* when Shaun is turned into a priest who is surrounded by twenty-nine schoolgirls who kiss his hands and make 'a tremendous girlsfuss over him ... and his rosyposy smile, mussing his frizzy hair and the golliwog curls of him'.[27] He may also be the model for the curate who, earlier, 'picks her up as gingerly as any balmbearer would to feel whereupon the virgin was most hurt and nicely asking: whyre have you been so grace a mauling and where were you chaste me child?'[28] Father Moran is not named in *Finnegans Wake*, but Joyce wrote in one of the notebooks he used when composing it: 'Fr Moran warned NB/not to frig.'[29]

Another Galway priest – a Jesuit – features prominently in *A Portrait of the Artist as a Young Man*, Joyce's semi-autobiographical novel about his days at school and university, and, more briefly, in *Ulysses*. The cruel prefect of studies at Clongowes Wood College in County Kildare, which Joyce entered as a boarder aged only six years, was Fr James Daly, a native of Ahascragh, near Ballinasloe, who had been educated by the Jesuits in Belgium before joining the order at the age of seventeen. Joyce called Daly 'Father Dolan' and 'Baldyhead Dolan' in the novel, where he recalled him entering the classroom asking, 'Any boys want flogging here?' before unjustly singling out the young Stephen Dedalus and caning him on both hands. The first strike, he wrote, 'made his trembling hand crumple together like a leaf in the fire' and the second one made his other hand 'shrink together with the palms and fingers in a livid quivering mass'.

Joyce's only authorised biographer Herbert Gorman described Daly as 'a born martinet' and 'a type who should never have been with the Society of Jesus'. He said he was 'the fire-snorting prefect of studies ... who flogged first and asked questions afterwards'.[30] For the reference to Father Dolan in *Ulysses* see Chapter 4.

Joyce teased Nora about her 'Galway priesteen' at the end of his 1912 visit to Galway when he returned to Dublin to find that his first poetry collection, *Chamber Music*, had been favourably reviewed in a Liverpool newspaper. He had left Nora in Galway while he tried to expedite the publication of *Dubliners*, but he wrote to her two days later asking about the 'priesteen' and also asking if such verses could be written by 'your friend in the soda water factory' – a reference to her last Galway boyfriend, Willie Mulvagh, who worked as an accountant in Joe Young's Mineral Water Company on Eglinton Street (now the Great Outdoors shop and adjoining nightclub premises). Mulvagh, renamed Mulvey to try perhaps to approximate the Galway pronunciation, is the Galway character who looms largest in *Ulysses* – see Chapter 4.

Joyce's question to Nora about whether the Galway 'priesteen' or her former Galway boyfriend could match his polished verses was a reference to the poems in *Chamber Music*, which were of sentimental value to both of them and which he sent her in a bound volume, handwritten in indelible ink on parchment paper, when they were apart at Christmas in 1909. He had been writing poetry before he met Nora and he installed her as his chief muse within weeks of their meeting. Three or four of the thirty-six poems in *Chamber Music* relate to Nora and at least two of them were written in the summer he met her. His first recorded words inspired by her, outside his letters to her, are in a poem he composed in the month after they met, including the lines:

Yet must thou fold me unaware
To know the rapture of thy heart

Another poem, written shortly before their elopement, is dedicated 'To Nora' and it ends with the line 'His love is his companion'. Another contains the line 'Love is unhappy when love is away!' that Joyce had engraved word for word on an ivory necklace he later had specially made for her. Yet another refers to the sundering of a key Joyce friendship after he had met Nora and distanced himself from former friends, including, most notably, the sometime Galway resident Oliver St John Gogarty, who later features prominently in his work (see Chapters 4 and 5).[31] Its two prophetic final lines are:

He is a stranger to me now
Who was my friend.

'I hope you liked the verses,' Joyce told Nora in another letter from Dublin to No. 4 Bowling Green. 'I spoke of you today to my aunt and told her of you – how you sit at the opera with the grey ribbon in your hair, listening to music, and observed by men, – and of many other things (even very intimate things) between us.'

3

LIPS

'Those strange places whose names thrill me on your lips,
Oughterard, Claregalway ... Oranmore'

As he walked thus through the ways of the city he had his ears
and eyes ever prompt to receive impressions.
— From *Stephen Hero*, Episode I

A LITTLE OVER THREE MONTHS after his first visit to Galway in 1909
Joyce wrote to Nora from Dublin: 'I leave for Cork tomorrow morning but I would prefer to be going westward, towards those strange
places whose names thrill me on your lips, Oughterard, Claregalway
... Oranmore.'[1]

His impulse to journey westward arose when he had to spend more
than ten weeks in Dublin overseeing the opening of a cinema – Ireland's
first – on behalf of four Italian businessmen he had met in Trieste. Nora
stayed behind in Trieste with young Giorgio and Lucia and he wrote to
her almost every day detailing how much he missed her.

He booked the Italians into Finn's Hotel and he persuaded one
of the waitresses to show him the room where Nora stayed while she
worked there. The visit to her former bedroom, at the back of the
building, intensified his already fierce longing for her. He told her that
he wished to travel westward, not just towards Oughterard and Oranmore, but 'towards those wild fields of Connacht in which God made
to grow "my beautiful wild flower of the hedges, my dark-blue rain-
drenched flower"'.

His longing for her intensified even further when he discovered that a young policeman who was helping to control the crowds at the newly opened cinema was from Galway. 'I *had* to speak to him because he came from Galway,' he told Nora, underlining the word 'had'.

> I took him upstairs to give him a drink and found he was from Galway and his sisters were at the Presentation Convent with you. He was amazed to hear where Nora Barnacle had ended. He said he remembered you in Galway, a handsome girl with curls and a proud walk.[2]

The mention of Nora's Galway past – which had inspired 'The Dead' and which would infuse much of Joyce's later poetry and prose – was enthralling and terrifying. 'My God, Nora, how I suffered!' he told her.

> Yet I could not stop talking to him. He seems a fine courteous-mannered young man. I wondered did my darling, my love, my dearest, my queen ever turn her young eyes towards him ... I am sure there are finer fellows in Galway than your poor lover but O, darling, one day you will see that I will be something in my country.[3]

'O, darling,' he went on, 'I am so jealous of the past and yet I bite my nails with excitement whenever I see anybody from the strange dying western city in which my love, my beautiful wild flower of the hedges, passed her young laughing girlish years.'

The 'strange dying western city' that Galway had become in the century following the Famine that is described in the letters Joyce wrote to his family and friends is also depicted memorably in the two lengthy, front-page articles he wrote for the Italian daily newspaper *Il Piccolo della Sera* a decade before he became famous.

The two newspaper articles dealing exclusively with Galway were written during his 1912 visit. They run to about 1,500 words each. One is about Galway city and the other is about the Aran Islands. Both drew heavily on James Hardiman's *History of the Town and County of Galway*, which was published in 1820 and which Joyce probably consulted in the city library. A study of translations of the articles by Kevin Barry, former Professor of English Literature at NUIG, found that 'a considerable amount' of Joyce's information came from Hardiman's history, with some passages 'almost wholly lifted from the footnotes'.[4]

The first article, 'The City of the Tribes', subtitled 'Italian Echoes in an Irish Port', was published on 11 August 1912, just four days after Joyce's visit to Ballybrit for the Galway Races. It teems with romance and history, highlighting the medieval links between Galway and mainland Europe.

'The signs on the corners of the narrow streets reflect the city's links with the Latin countries of Europe,' he wrote, 'Madeira Street, Merchant Street, Spaniards Walk, Madeira Island, Lombard Street, Velasquez de Palmeira Avenue.' Oliver Cromwell, he noted, had acknowledged that 'the port of Galway was the United Kingdom's second most important harbour, and the main market in the entire Kingdom for Spanish and Italian commerce'.

The waters of Galway Bay 'were ploughed by thousands of foreign ships' in the Middle Ages, Joyce wrote, adding that 'almost all the wine imported into the United Kingdom from the kingdoms of Spain, Portugal, the Canary Islands and Italy passed through this port'.

Joyce noted that evidence of the strong links between Italy and Galway in its medieval heyday included the appointment of a Florentine merchant, Andrea Gerardo, as a government tax collector in the city in the fourteenth century and one Giovanni Fante being named as a city official in the seventeenth century.

He continued:

The city's protector is Saint Nicholas of Bari and the so-called 'seal of the college' bears the effigy of this saint who is the patron saint of sailors and children. The papal envoy, Cardinal Rinuccini, came to Galway during the trial of the martyr king, and placed the city under the papal flag. The clergy and religious orders refused to recognize his authority, so the hot-headed Cardinal broke the bell in Carmelite Church, and placed two of his own loyal priests at the church door to stop the faithful from getting in.

Two further strong Italian links were preserved, he wrote, in the parish house of Saint Nicholas (adjacent to Bowling Green; now demolished and replaced by a car park). One is an autographed letter from Pope Alexander VI, a member of the Borgia family, and the other is 'a curious document, left by an Italian traveller in the 16th Century, in which the writer says that wherever he had travelled in the world, never had he seen in the blink of an eye what he saw when he arrived in Galway – a priest raising the Host, a pack chasing a little deer, a ship entering the port under full sail, and a salmon being killed with a lance'.

Nearly half of the article dealt with the 'Tribes of Galway', particularly the Lynches, whom Joyce deemed 'the most famous of all the tribes' and whose residence he described as 'the sad and dark castle that still darkens the main street'.[5] He devoted nearly a quarter of the essay to the retelling of the notorious story associated with the Lynch Window on Market Street, which he could see from Nora Barnacle's front door on Bowling Green (and which is still visible from there). Joyce wrote that the reputed hanging by Mayor James Lynch of his only son, Walter, at that window in 1493 after the son had been found guilty of the murder of a Spanish nobleman whose safety in Galway the father had guaranteed, was 'the most tragic thing recorded in the city's history'.

His retelling, borrowed almost entirely from an account in Hardiman's history, concluded: 'Then the father himself hanged his son from the window beam in front of the eyes of the terrified crowd.' The alleged murder victim had been a love rival of the Lynch son and the tale allowed Joyce to claim, without attribution, that: 'In Galway city, wrote an ancient chronicler, the passions of pride and lust reigned supreme.'

Hardiman, writing at the beginning of the nineteenth century, did not regard the Lynch Window story as apocryphal and he devoted eight pages of his history to it. He acknowledged that most of the received versions 'are the offspring of fancy', but he added that 'this by no means affects the truth of the principal occurrence'.[6] He also commissioned an artist to prepare an engraving of the 'House in Galway, out of which the Mayor executed his son, with the ancient monument over the door'. The 'ancient monument' is the skull and crossbones that can still be seen on the Lynch Memorial Window on Market Street.[7]

However, a more recent distinguished historian, the late Professor T. P. O'Neill, lecturer and Associate Professor of History at University College Galway between 1967 and 1987, and a biographer of Éamon de Valera, came to a different conclusion. During Galway's quincentennial celebrations in 1984, which he initiated, O'Neill wrote:

> Perhaps it is a pity that the most famous Lynch story of all is a piece of fiction – that is the tale about the Mayor who hanged his own son. A monument to this non-event, the front wall of a house where it never happened, has for years been one of the most visited sites in the city.[8]

Whatever the truth about what actually happened at the Lynch Window in the centuries before its transfer to Market Street, Joyce noted the contrast between ancient Galway's medieval glory and its decrepit and decaying state in 1912 in his article's opening and closing paragraphs. 'The old Spanish houses are in ruins, and weeds have taken hold in the frames of their dirty windows,' he wrote. 'The castles of the tribes are crumbling ... weeds grow in the windows and in the wide courtyards. Over the portals, the illustrious coats of arms, etched in the darkened rock, have faded ...'[9]

Faded too, he observed, was any evidence to support the widespread belief that 'Galway's inhabitants are descendants of Spanish stock and that you only have to take a few steps into the ancient city's gloomy alleyways to meet the typical olive-skinned, raven-haired Spanish type'. The black eyes and raven hair of the old Spanish stock was now 'scarce enough', he noted, 'since a Titian red is more a preponderance'.

Joyce's description of the city centre – and he spent most of his two visits based either in Bowling Green or Dominic Street – contrasts with his impression of the suburbs. The city, he wrote, 'lies among innumerable little islands, veined in every direction by rivulets, cataracts, streams, and canals', but the environs were far less attractive. 'Outside the city walls', he observed, 'the suburbs have flourished – new, bright and oblivious of the past, but you have only to close your eyes to this irritating modernity for a moment to see in the dim light of history "the Spanish city".'

One area outside the city walls that was anything but burdened by bothersome modernity in 1912 was the Claddagh. Joyce noticed its whitewashed and thatched cottages as he sailed out of the harbour towards Inishmor to gather material for his article on the Aran Islands. 'A cluster of hovels, but nonetheless a kingdom' was how he described the Claddagh, adding:

> Up until a few years ago the village elected its own king, had it own costumes, made its own laws and lived apart from the rest. The wedding rings worn by its inhabitants are to this day adorned with the seal of the king: two hands joined together and holding a crowned heart.

He also accurately described the Claddagh tradition of the blessing of the bay each August:

> Every year on the eve of the August fair, when the herring fishing begins, the waters of the bay are blessed. The flotilla of small fishing leaves from the Claddagh, led by a flagship on whose deck stands a Dominican friar. When it has reached an appropriate point, the flotilla stops, the fishermen kneel and

uncover their heads and the padre, murmuring prayers to ward off bad luck, shakes his aspergill on the waters and makes the sign of the cross in the dark air.

Less accurate, however, was his claim that the bay contained the wrecks of many Spanish Armada ships, or his suggestion that their surviving shipwrecked sailors were universally welcomed in Galway when they scrambled ashore. He wrote:

> The peasants of County Galway, remembering the long friendship between Spain and Ireland, hid the fugitives from the vengeance of the English garrison and wrapped their shipwrecked dead in white sheets and gave them a sacred burial.[10]

Beyond the Claddagh on his right Joyce viewed the beaches of Silver Strand, Barna and Furbo, while his travelling companion – probably Nora's uncle Michael Healy – told him of the plans to build a new transatlantic port there to offer the shortest crossing between Europe and the United States and Canada. Joyce retained some of this information for use in *Ulysses* (see Chapter 4), but he likened the plan to the mirage of the Aran fisherman who hoped to follow the legendary voyage of Saint Brendan the Navigator across the Atlantic Ocean and he titled his article 'The Mirage of the Fisherman of Aran'.

Joyce mentioned Christopher Columbus, but he ignored his supposed visit to Galway en route to his 'discovery' of America, favouring instead Saint Brendan's voyage from the Aran Islands as the pioneering one. 'A thousand years before the sailor from Genova was laughed at in Salamanca, Saint Brendan set sail for the New World from the austere shore to which our ship is now headed and, after crossing the ocean, he arrived at the coast of Florida,' he wrote.

On Inishmor, where 'it rains like it only knows how to rain in Ireland', Joyce saw that the rocks were 'covered with purple and reddish seaweed, commonly seen in the shops of the greengrocers in Galway' and he noted the distinctive dress and footwear of the fishermen, the latter for later use in *Ulysses* (see Chapter 4). 'The Aran fisherman is sure of foot,' he wrote. 'He wears a rough flat sandal of untanned oxhide, open at the arch, with no heels and tied with rawhide laces. He dresses in wool, thick like felt, and wears a black wide-brimmed hat.'

Joyce saw the islanders he met as people from a 'bygone civilization', mysterious and shy. He mentioned former inhabitants, including the island's patron, Saint Enda, 'the visionary Saint Fursa' and Saint Finnian, who 'left here to become bishop of Lucca'. He added: 'Aran, it is said, is the strangest place in the world.' His companion offered money to an old woman who had invited them into her home for tea and bread, but she rejected the offer 'almost in anger and asks us if we are trying to dishonour her house'.

One of the people Joyce met on Inishmor was a man named O'Flaherty, a surname he described as 'a princely name' and 'the name which the young Oscar Wilde proudly had printed on the cover of his first book'. Joyce devoted a full article to Oscar Wilde in *Il Piccolo della Sera* in March 1909, six months before his first visit to Galway, and Wilde's play *The Importance of Being Earnest* was the first one staged by Joyce and his exiled troupe of players in Zurich in 1918.

Wilde's full name was Oscar Fingal O'Flahertie Wills Wilde, the O'Flahertie name being included to honour the Galway connections of his father, the renowned surgeon and antiquarian Sir William Wilde. Sir William owned the imposing house Moytura, which overlooks and is still visible from the middle lake on Lough Corrib. The young Wilde spent his holidays at Moytura, and he accompanied his father on some of the field trips that led to Sir William Wilde's seminal 1867 book *Lough Corrib, Its Shores and Islands*. It was outside Sir William Wilde's Dublin home, No. 1 Merrion Square, that Joyce and Nora Barnacle met for their first date.

Oscar Wilde's Galway connection allowed Joyce to refer in his *Il Piccolo della Sera* article to the famous inscription on one of the city's medieval gates – 'from the ferocious O'Flahertys O Lord deliver us'. Joyce wrote that the O'Flaherties were 'a fierce Irish tribe whose destiny it was to attack the gates of medieval cities, instilling terror into peaceful people, and even now they recite at the end of the ancient litany of the saints, in times of pestilence, or the wrath of God or in the spirit of fornication: "from the fierce O'Flaherties, *libera nos Domine.*"

Another bloody episode in Galway's history was the basis of an article Joyce published in *Ill Piccolo della Sera* two years before his first visit to the city. In contending that international public opinion on Ireland was mediated and distorted through the British establishment and British newspapers, he cited the 'sensational trial' and executions that followed the Maamtrasna murders in Connemara, 'a lonely place in a western province', in 1882, the year of his own birth.

The trial was transferred from Galway to Dublin at the request of the Crown and it was conducted entirely in English, although the accused understood only Irish. The prime suspect and the oldest of the accused was seventy-year-old Myles Joyce. 'Public opinion at the time judged him innocent and these days considers him a martyr,' wrote Joyce. He continued:

> The court had to use the services of an interpreter. The questioning which this man translated was at times comic and at times tragic. On the one hand was the stiff officious interpreter and on the other the patriarch of this wretched tribe who, unused to civic customs, seemed quite bewildered by all the legal ceremonies. The image of this bewildered old man, left over from a culture that is not ours, deaf and mute in front of his judge, is the symbolic image of the Irish nation at the bar of public opinion.

Myles Joyce and his two co-accused were sentenced to be hanged following a six-day trial at Green Street Courthouse. The jury took only six minutes to convict Myles Joyce. Sworn statements to a magistrate by Myles Joyce's two co-accused insisting on his innocence were suppressed. The executions, less than four months after the murders, took place in the grounds of Galway jail (now the Cathedral car park). 'The square in front of the prison was hiving with people who on bended knee called out prayers in Irish for the repose of Myles Joyce's soul,' wrote Joyce. He added: 'Legend has it that not even the hangman could make himself understood to Joyce and, getting frustrated, kicked the unhappy man in the head to make his head go into the noose.'[11]

This gruesome story stayed with Joyce and he returned to it in *Finnegans Wake*, doubtless because the victims and some of the accused came from 'the ancient tribe of the Joyces' and because the events took place in the year he was born.

Joyce's articles on the Maamtrasna murders and on Oscar Wilde were written before he visited Galway, but after he had begun living with Nora Barnacle. Before he met her, however, his knowledge of Galway and Galwegians was as faulty and incomplete as 'the lazy Dubliner' he would condemn in his 'City of the Tribes' article, 'who travels little and knows his country only by what he hears'.

One of his first published pieces – written more than six and a half years before his own first journey west of the Shannon, and fifteen months before he had first met Nora Barnacle – portrayed west of Ireland people half-jokingly and unflatteringly. The piece was a review in the *Daily Express* in March 1903 of a just-published book by Lady Gregory of Coole Park, *Poets and Dreamers: Studies & Translations from the Irish*.

Joyce, barely twenty-one years of age, wrote that half of Lady Gregory's book was 'an account of old men and old women in the West of Ireland'; he went on:

> These old people are full of stories about giants and witches, and bogs and black-handled knives, and they tell their stories one after another at great length and with many repetitions (for they are people of leisure) by the fire or in the yard of a workhouse. It is difficult to judge well of their charms and herb-healing, for that is the province of those who are learned in these matters and can compare the customs of countries,

and, indeed, it is well not to know these magical-sciences, for if the wind changes while you are cutting wild camomile you will lose your mind.

(This is Joyce's interpretation of Lady Gregory's account in her book of what she had been told by a well-known herb-healer from near Gort, Bridget Ruane, about gathering wild camomile or ribgrass.)

In the review Joyce also referred to Anthony Raftery, the nineteenth-century wandering blind poet (Raifteiraí an File), who spent most of his life around Gort in south Galway – including at Ballylee, where William Butler Yeats later lived – and who is buried in Killeenin, on the road between Craughwell and Kilcolgan, under a gravestone funded by Lady Gregory (see Chapter 7). Raftery, who died ten years before the start of the Famine, was the subject of the first chapter in Lady Gregory's book, an essay of over 13,500 words in which she included the reminiscences of some of his friends and neighbours and translations from Irish of some of his poems, as well as an account of his funeral. Her book also contains several other references to Raftery, as well as a translation of a Douglas Hyde play about him, *An Posadh* (The Marriage), and she was centrally involved in arranging for a commemorative slab to be placed over his previously unmarked grave in 1900, at a ceremony attended by herself and W.B. Yeats. It's likely that Joyce first learned about Raftery in Lady Gregory's book and he referred to him again in *Ulysses*, where in Episode 9 he compares the 'delightful lovesongs' of the Gaelic League founder Douglas Hyde to 'the harsher and more personal note which is found in the satirical effusions of the famous Raftery'.

Elsewhere in the *Daily Express* review, which Joyce later acknowledged as 'very severe' in a letter to his mother, he repeated Lady Gregory's claim that Raftery, who spent much of his life moving from patron to patron, was the last of the great Irish bardic poets. He also repeated her version of Raftery's own poetic account of taking shelter from a shower of rain near Headford on the banks of the Corrib: 'He took shelter one day from the rain under a bush: at first the bush

kept out the rain, and he made verses praising it, but after a while it
let the rain through, and he made verses dispraising it.' (As well as
the play about Raftery, Lady Gregory included translations of three
other Douglas Hyde plays in *Poets and Dreamers*. Hyde's *Love Songs
of Connaught* (1893) and four books by Lady Gregory were among the
hundreds of books Joyce left behind him in Trieste when he moved
to Paris in 1920.)

Most of Joyce's other observations about Galway did not emerge
until many years after his death, when letters that were bequeathed to
libraries or purchased from his relatives and friends were published.
These letters are now preserved in libraries in Yale, Harvard, Buffalo, Cornell, Texas, Kansas and Southern Illinois, as well as Dublin,
London and Zurich.

Among them is a letter-card Joyce sent to Nora during his first
Galway visit in 1909 and written in her mother's kitchen in Bowling
Green:

> My dear little runaway Nora, I am writing this to you sitting at
> the kitchen table in your mother's house! I have been here all
> day talking with her and I see that she is my darling's mother
> and I like her very much. ... I shall stay in Galway overnight. ...
> I went round to the house in Augustine Street where you lived
> with your grandmother and in the morning I am going to visit
> it pretending I want to buy it in order to see the room you slept
> in ... next year you and I may come here. You will take me from
> place to place and the image of your girlhood will purify again
> my life.[12]

The letter-card (a letter-cum-postcard) was illustrated with
images of the Claddagh, Salthill, Menlo Castle, St Ignatius Church
(Sea Road) and the Claddagh Church interior.

Some of Joyce's ventures outside Galway city are described in a
letter he sent from Bowling Green to his brother Stanislaus in 1912,

beginning with a futile trip to Clifden to try to interview the Italian émigré Guglielmo Marconi. Marconi had established the world's first wireless telegraphy station there in 1907:

> I went to Clifden on Monday to interview Marconi or see station. Could do neither and am waiting reply from Marconi House London. ... I think since I have come so far I had better stay a little longer if possible. Nora's uncle feeds us in great style and I row and cycle and drive a good deal. I cycled to Oughterard on Sunday and visited the graveyard of 'The Dead'. It is exactly as I imagined it and one of the headstones was to J. Joyce.

He stayed in Galway for another ten days before returning to Dublin to try again to expedite publication of *Dubliners*, the short story collection that ends with 'The Dead'. He left Nora in Galway with the children, but he wrote to her every day, pouring out his frustrations over continuing obstructions to the publication of his work:

> You are away in Galway. I don't know how we will get back to Trieste or what we shall find there. I don't know what to do ... I told you of my grief at Galway Races. I feel it still. I hope that the day may come when I shall be able to give you the fame of being beside me when I have entered into my Kingdom.

Ten more years of struggle and poverty lay ahead of Joyce and Nora before they began to experience the onset of the fame – and infamy – that followed the publication of *Ulysses*. The book's success, despite an unwritten ban for many years on its sale in Ireland, and a full ban in England and the United States for nearly a dozen years, prompted Nora to return to Galway for the first time in ten years, but the visit – her last – was ruined and foreshortened by an eruption of violence presaging the outbreak of the Civil War.

Rival factions of the sundering IRA were grappling for possession of Galway's key buildings and armed soldiers were billeted in various hotels when she arrived home with Giorgio and Lucia in April 1922.

Joyce, who was always exceptionally frightened of war and violence, strongly opposed Nora's visit home and he fulminated about it for years afterwards. He persuaded Nora to delay in London for a week, but she wanted the now-teenage children to see their grandparents in Galway and Dublin. The success of the first edition of *Ulysses* – published in Paris on 2 February, Joyce's fortieth birthday, and quickly sold out – brought her a steady supply of cash for the first time in the eighteen years since she left Galway.

The Civil War was only weeks away when she arrived home. Anti-Treaty forces had ejected their former colleagues from Renmore Barracks at the beginning of the month and an IRA officer was shot and badly wounded outside the Railway Hotel (now the Meyrick) a few days later.

'About midnight', the *Connacht Tribune* reported, 'the citizens were startled by a sudden burst of revolver firing which recalled the months of terror when the Black and Tans were in charge of the streets at night.' The Galway to Dublin train was stopped and rifled by armed men at Oranmore. Post offices were robbed and cars were stolen almost every day as the violence escalated in the city and county.

Éamon de Valera, the leader of the anti-Treaty faction, addressed large meetings in Gort, Tuam, Oughterard and Galway city over the symbolic Easter weekend of 22 and 23 April, warning in each speech that the Dáil vote in favour of the Anglo-Irish Treaty the previous December had brought the country to the 'verge of civil war'.

Nora and the children fled from Galway after soldiers forcefully took over their lodgings. They left hurriedly by train while Joyce was contemplating sending a private aircraft to rescue them, but they had to dive for cover on the train as it passed through a gun battle outside Renmore Barracks.

'The air in Galway is very good but dear at the present price' was Joyce's mildest reference to his wife's native city in his accounts of her last visit there.[13] He was still angry and upset that 'what I had foreseen took place' when he wrote to his aunt Josephine more than six months later.

He told her:

> In Galway my son was dogged about the streets and, as he told me, he could not sleep at night with the thought that the Zulus, as he calls them, would taken him out of bed and shoot him. A drunken officer swaggered up to him blocking the path and asked him: 'How does it feel to be a gentleman's son?' ... The warehouse opposite their lodgings in Galway was seized by rebels, Free State troops invaded their bedrooms and planted machine guns in the windows. They ran through the town to the station and escaped in a train, lying flat on their bellies (the two females that is) amid a fusillade which continued for an hour from right and left between the troops on the train and ambushes along the line ... no doubt you will see Nora some other time when she goes to revisit her native dunghill though it is doubtful if Giorgio and Lucia will go.[14]

Ten years later the memory had still not faded. Explaining to his friend the poet T.S. Eliot why he never returned to Ireland, he wrote: 'When my wife and children went there in 1922, against my wish, they had to flee for their lives, lying flat on the floor of a railway carriage while rival parties shot at each other across their heads ...'[15]

He mentioned the ordeal again three years later when Nora was considering a repeat trip to Galway to see her mother, who was then nearing eighty years of age. 'I suppose it is only right,' he told his main benefactor, Harriet Weaver, before adding: 'The last time, however, she went there she left that blissful isle lying on the floor of a railway carriage with her two children (and mine) while the natives were firing at one another through the carriage windows.'[16]

These complaints were the only times that Joyce went close to disparaging Nora's native place. They carry traces, however, of the testy remark of the alter ego Gabriel Conroy in 'The Dead' when the 'frank-mannered' Molly Ivors was trying to entice him to join an excursion to the Aran Islands and reminding him that his wife Gretta was 'from Connacht'. He replied curtly: 'Her people are.'

4

MULVEY

'The only rock in Galway Bay'

What had Gretta Conroy on?
— Leopold Bloom, *Ulysses* (4:522)

He put his lines together not word by word but letter by letter.
— *Stephen Hero*, Episode XVI

His judgment was exquisite, deliberate, sharp; his sentence sculptural ... Like an alchemist he bent upon his handiwork, bringing together the mysterious elements, separating the subtle from the gross. For the artist the rhythms of phrase and period, the symbols of word and allusion, were paramount things ... To those multitudes not as yet in the wombs of humanity but surely engenderable there, he would give the word.
— *A Portrait of the Artist*[1]

Let him find
News of his dear father where he may
And win his own renown about the world
— Homer, *The Odyssey*, Book One, 120-3

GALWAY AND CONNEMARA ARE MENTIONED several times in *Ulysses*, the Joyce masterwork that is widely regarded as the greatest novel written in the English language.[2]

Throughout the epic Joyce retells many tales he had heard from Nora Barnacle, or her family, resulting in mentions of Galway, Galwegians or Connemara in fourteen of the book's eighteen chapters (or episodes, as Joyce preferred to call them).

'Of all the people who made *Ulysses* possible, the most important is Nora Barnacle,' wrote Harvard University literary historian Kevin Birmingham in 2014.[3] He added that the date of her first evening with Joyce – 16 June 1904 – 'hovers over everything that happens in *Ulysses*'. The most eminent Joyce biographer and scholar, Richard Ellmann, agreed. 'Joyce remembered the date with sacramental precision,' he observed, adding: 'He encouraged his admirers to call it "Bloomsday".'[4]

The novel's first and last lines carry echoes of Galway. Its very first four words – 'Stately, plump Buck Mulligan' – refer to Oliver St John Gogarty, a sometime Joyce friend who had very strong Galway connections (see Chapter 5), and its final lines – where Molly Bloom recalls being kissed 'under the Moorish wall' – have been linked to Nora Barnacle's recollections of being courted in Galway, near the Spanish Arch.[5]

The first words spoken by any character are Mulligan's Latin Mass *Introibo* and the last spoken words are Molly's. In those final words Molly refers to herself as 'a Flower of the mountain' and 'my mountain flower', copying Joyce's own oft-repeated words to Nora in several letters he wrote to her when they were apart. The Molly monologue that fills the novel's last sixty-two pages is based on Nora's speaking and writing style. 'Do you notice how women when they write disregard stops and capital letters?' Joyce asked his brother Stanislaus in a letter accompanied by a note from Nora that illustrated his point.[6] Joyce also said that Molly's monologue was the book's 'star turn'.[7]

The opening episode of *Ulysses* is set in a Martello Tower in Sandycove, south Dublin (now a James Joyce museum), which Oliver St John Gogarty rented and where he and Joyce briefly lived together with another friend of Gogarty in the summer of 1904, shortly before Joyce eloped with Nora. Gogarty is renamed Malachi Mulligan by

Joyce in *Ulysses* and, as Mulligan, he recites three verses of his own poem 'The Song of the Cheerful (but slightly sarcastic) Jazus' (retitled 'The ballad of Joking Jesus' by Joyce) in the opening episode before reappearing prominently in several later episodes.[8]

Mulligan's aunt, or 'the aunt' as she is called in a number of mentions from page two onwards, was Galway-born Annie Oliver – an unmarried sister of Gogarty's mother Margaret – who lived in the Gogarty household in Dublin when Oliver was growing up (see Chapter 5).

The novel's central couple, Leopold and Molly Bloom, have a Connemara Marble clock on the mantelpiece of their home at No. 7 Eccles Street (where the Mater Private Hospital now stands). The clock, which they received as a wedding present, had stopped at 4.46 a.m. on 21 March 1896, Nora Barnacle's twelfth birthday, the last before she became a teenager.[9] (Another example of how 'Joyce would not waste any stone on just one bird', as Fritz Senn has observed in another context.[10])

And Molly in her famous soliloquy recalls giving a Claddagh Ring to an old lover, Lieutenant Stanley Gardner, who was killed in the Boer War in South Africa. She says the ring 'must have been pure 16 carat gold because it was very heavy'.

Molly's former lovers – real and suspected – haunt Leopold Bloom in much the same way that Nora Barnacle's young Galway loves disquieted James Joyce, an obsession already manifest in his letters to her and in 'The Dead', *Exiles* and 'She Weeps Over Rahoon'.

Molly's most remembered erstwhile lover, Harry Mulvey, is based on Nora's last love before she met Joyce and he is the Galway character who looms largest in the novel.[11] Although never seen and referred to mostly only by his surname, Mulvey haunts Molly and her husband throughout the second half of *Ulysses*. Leopold Bloom mentions Mulvey (who he has never met) four times before Molly wallows at length in memories of her passionate times with him. It was Mulvey who gave her the Claddagh ring 'for luck' that she later passed on to Lieutenant Gardner.

Like Michael Furey in 'The Dead', Lieutenant Mulvey is a fictional composite of the young Galway loves that Nora told Joyce about; however, he is modelled mainly on her last Galway boyfriend, Willie Mulvagh, from Newtownsmith, which adjoins Bowling Green. Nora left Galway after one of her uncles violently broke up her liaison with Willie Mulvagh, because his family were Protestants (Church of Ireland). One of Nora's childhood friends, Kathleen O'Halloran, told the Joyce biographer Richard Ellmann that she and Nora would pretend they were going out walking in the evening, but that she would sit and wait in the Abbey Church on Francis Street while Nora spent time with Mulvagh.[12] She said: 'Then one night Nora was caught ... her uncle Tommy he followed her down till she went in home and he gave her a bad beating. The following week she left for Dublin.'

The real Willie Mulvagh was the eldest son of a Royal Irish Constabulary pensioner who had been stationed in Galway as a policeman. Willie had moved out of the family home in Newstownsmith when the 1901 census was taken and he was working as an accountant in Joe Young's Mineral Water Company on Eglinton Street (now the Great Outdoors shop and adjoining premises) when he went out with Nora. 'Can your friend in the soda water factory ... write my verses?' Joyce asked her in a letter after he had been living with her for eight years.[13]

'Assuming Mulvey to be the first ...' muses Leopold Bloom, displaying similar jealousy. Earlier, in similar vein, he says: 'Molly, lieutenant Mulvey that kissed her under the Moorish wall beside the gardens. Fifteen she told me.'

'Mulveys was the first,' confirms Molly in her soliloquy, ensuring that the trysts between Nora Barnacle and Willie Mulvagh in turn-of-the-century Galway would enter literary history. 'I knew more about men and life when I was 15 than they'll all know at 50,' she adds.

Nor was Nora's sentimentality over Willie Mulvagh – so strong that Joyce was still writing about it almost twenty years after the liaison – one-sided. One of Mulvagh's sisters, Hetty, told the Nora biographer Padraic O Laoi that Willie had really loved Nora and that he had been heartbroken when she left Galway abruptly. But his daughter, Evelyn Mulvagh Odierna, told another biographer, Brenda Maddox, that

Willie had lived the rest of his life in complete ignorance of his role in the dominant literary work of the twentieth century (albeit a work that was effectively unobtainable in Galway or elsewhere in Ireland for most of that century).

Evelyn Mulvagh told Maddox that in old age her father had looked up from a newspaper he was reading and had asked: 'James Joyce? Didn't he marry a Galway girl by the name of Barnacle?'[14]

Nora Barnacle is also likely to have alerted Joyce to another Galway story that he could not resist including in *Ulysses* – the mysterious grounding of a passenger ship on the Margaretta Rock, off Knocknacarra, in 1858. The date of the grounding, 16 June, was too much of a coincidence for him to ignore and he referred to it in two episodes of the novel he set in Dublin forty-six years later.

Joyce would have known from Nora and her family that suspicions persisted in Galway that the grounded ship, the *Indian Empire*, had been deliberately steered onto the Margaretta Rock by two pilots hired in England in order to prevent Galway from becoming established as the major transatlantic port in Britain and Ireland. The pilots were arrested and charged, but one of them died suddenly while awaiting trial, fuelling the already-strong rumours that they had been bribed to scuttle the ship by people one Galway newspaper described as 'certain Liverpool interests'.

Early in *Ulysses*, in Episode 2, the Dalkey schoolmaster Mr Garrett Deasy mentions 'the Liverpool ring which jockeyed the Galway harbour scheme' in his litany of the wrongs suffered by Ireland.[15] The incident is mentioned again in Episode 16 when the keeper of a late-night cabman's shelter at Butt Bridge, near the Custom House, asks his customers aloud 'why that ship ran bang against the only rock in Galway Bay when the Galway harbour scheme was mooted ... ?' The keeper adds: 'Ask her captain ... how much palm oil the British Government gave him for that day's work?'

The keeper then names 'Captain John Lever of the Lever line', referring to John Orrell Lever, the Manchester businessman who had chartered the *Indian Empire* and who was planning to use it to establish a transatlantic service from Galway. Lever, who later became Conservative MP for Galway, was the subject of unsubstantiated innuendo in Galway that he would have profited from an insurance policy if the *Indian Empire* had foundered and even that he had hired the two pilots who were on board when it hit the rock.

The keeper's mention of John Lever prompts the drunken, red-bearded sailor in the shelter, W. B. Murphy, to sing boisterously:

> *The biscuits was as hard as brass,*
> *And the beef as salt as Lot's wife's arse.*
> *O Johnny Lever!*
> *Johnny Lever, O!*

Also in the night shelter at the time was Leopold Bloom, and he too 'had a very shrewd suspicion that Mr Johnny Lever got rid of some £.s.d. in the course of his perambulations round the docks in the congenial atmosphere of the *Old Ireland* tavern, come back to Erin and so on'.

The *Indian Empire* grounding was certainly mysterious, and it undoubtedly damaged Galway's prospects of becoming a major trans-atlantic seaport, causing innuendo to linger in Galway. However, Joyce's two references to it in *Ulysses* rely on the rumours, not the facts. (For more details see Chapter 6.)

Galway's earlier maritime decline is lamented in Episode 12, 'Cyclops', by the character named only as 'the Citizen', who is mod-elled on Michael Cusack, one of the founders of the GAA and the man after whom the Cusack Stand in Croke Park and Cusack Park in Ennis are named. (Cusack Park is accessed by walking past the Queen's Hotel, which in *Ulysses* was owned by Bloom's father, Rudolph, who took his own life there with an overdose of toxins purchased in a local chemist's shop in a 'redlabelled bottle'. A large bronze statue of Michael Cusack stands under the entrance to the Cusack Stand in Croke Park and a plaque marks the house he lived in on Gardiner Place, off Mountjoy Square near Croke Park.)

Blaming the British for Ireland's 'ruined trade', the Citizen says:

We had our trade with Spain and the French and with the Flemings before those mongrels were pupped, Spanish ale in Galway, the winebark on the winedark waterday ... And with the help of the holy mother of God we will again ... Our harbours that are empty will be full again, Queenstown, Kinsale, Galway, Blacksod Bay, Ventry in the kingdom of Kerry, Killybegs, the third largest harbour in the wide world, with a fleet of masts of the Galway Lynches and the Cavan O'Reillys and the O'Kennedy's of Dublin.

The Galway Lynches feature again when Lynch's Castle on Shop Street is among the ancient Irish beauty spots 'intricately embroidered' on the Citizen's handkerchief, along with Glen Inagh and the Twelve Pins in Connemara and Croagh Patrick, which is visible from parts of Galway, as is Cong Abbey, which is just over the Galway/Mayo border at Ashford Castle. A medical student who makes a number of appearances is given the surname Lynch after the Galway tribe.

The Citizen also blames the British – 'the yellowjohns of Anglia' – for ending the export to other countries of Irish produce that is 'second to none', including 'Connemara marble' and 'our farfamed horses' and for cutting down 'the giant ash of Galway' and other trees of Ireland.

The names of the Connemara offshore islands of Inishboffin, Inishturk and Inishark are heard by Leopold Bloom through an open window of St Joseph's National School on Upper Dorset Street as they are recited by the schoolboys at geography class while he walks to the pork butcher's to buy food for breakfast.

'The windy wilds of Connemara' and the Aran Islands are cited among certain localities of 'attractive character' in Ireland, and there are references elsewhere to 'the wilds of Connemara', 'the Connemara hills' and 'all the goats in Connemara'.

'The tramper Synge' mentioned in Episode 9, set in the National Library (where the banisters on the ornate main staircase, or 'curving balustrade' in Joyce's words, are of Connemara marble), is the playwright and sometime Aran Islands-resident John Millington Synge. 'He's out in pampooties to murder you,' Buck Mulligan tells the Joyce character, Stephen Dedalus. Pampooties are the cowhide footwear of the Aran Islanders of the twentieth century and of Synge's Aran Island play *Riders to the Sea*.

Synge's writing style in *Riders to the Sea* and his other plays is wickedly parodied by Joyce, via Mulligan, as he teases Stephen: 'It's what I'm telling you, mister Honey, it's queer and sick we were ... and we one hour and two hours and three hours in Connery's sitting civil waiting for pints apiece ... and we to be there, mavrone, and you to be unbeknownst sending us your conglomerations the way we have our tongues out a yard long like the drouthy clerics do be fainting for a pussful.' And later, he adds: '*Pogue mahone! Achushla machree!* It's destroyed we are from this day! It's destroyed we are surely!' Joyce mocked Synge's style again in a later episode when a ghost mutters: 'This is the appearance is on me. Tare and ages, what way would I be resting at all and I tramping Dublin this while back with my share of songs.'

Mulligan/Gogarty also teases Stephen/Joyce in the National Library about Lady Gregory of Coole Park, outside Gort, who had secured Joyce's first regular work, reviewing books for the Dublin *Daily Express*, only to find that his first review was a dismissal of her own latest book, which was mostly about Galway people and history. In a reference to the dismissive review of the book, *Poets and Dreamers*, Mulligan says the *Daily Express* editor is 'awfully sick' after 'what you wrote about that old hake Gregory'. He adds: 'She gets you a job on the paper and you go and slate her drivel to Jaysus. Couldn't you do the Yeats touch?' – a reference to W.B. Yeats' description of the book as 'beautiful' in a review entitled 'The Galway Plains' from his 1903 essay collection *Ideas of Good and Evil* (A.H. Bullen, London). He teases Stephen further by parodying the words of Yeats, who was a close friend of Lady Gregory and a regular guest at Coole Park: 'The most beautiful book that has come out of our country in my time.'

The two west of Ireland people to whom Lady Gregory devoted most pages in *Poets and Dreamers* – the Gaelic League founder and future President of Ireland Douglas Hyde and the wandering poet Anthony Raftery – are mentioned in the same breath by the unseen narrator of the scene dominated by the Citizen in Barney Kiernan's pub.[16] Referring to 'ancient Celtic bards', the narrator says:

> We are not speaking so much of those delightful lovesongs with which the writer who conceals his identity under the graceful pseudonym of the Little Sweet Branch has familiarized the bookloving world but rather ... of the harsher and more personal note which is found in the satirical effusions of the famous Raftery.

A reference to Gort – 'Goodbye Ireland I'm going to Gort' – in the same episode seems not to be a reference to Lady Gregory, but rather an oblique way of saying 'I'm going out' or 'I'm going to the toilet' (*gort* being the Irish word for field or park). Slieve Aughty, which rises near the mansion Roxborough House, where Lady Gregory was born and reared, is mentioned among other mountains and hills on which tar barrels and bonfires were lit.

Two other nineteenth-century Galway aristocrats also appear unflatteringly. The 'two Ardilauns' that are ordered in Burke's pub, after Mulligan, Stephen and others have emerged from an evening of drinking in the nearby National Maternity Hospital, signify two bottles or two pints of Guinness; this is a reference to Lord Ardilaun of Ashford Castle, County Galway, co-owner of the Guinness brewery with his brother Lord Iveagh.[17]

Lord Ardilaun (1840–1915) was the Dublin-born Arthur Edward Guinness, a great-grandson of the first Arthur Guinness, founder of the famous brewery. He was made Baron Ardilaun of Ashford in 1880 when he lost his House of Commons seat for Dublin in a general election (he was given the news of his defeat at the count by James Joyce's father, John, who claimed to have helped unseat him through his campaigning for rival candidates). Lord Ardilaun oversaw extensive renovations to Ashford Castle, which borders Joyce Country, and he built the castle approach bridge which straddles the border between counties Galway and Mayo; the large carved letter 'A' on it refers to him. He also owned other large tracts of land in County Galway and he was part-owner for a time of the Aran Islands.

The title Ardilaun is taken from Ard Oilean (High Island), one of the islands on the upper lake of Lough Corrib, near Ashford Castle. Lord Ardilaun was also for a time the owner of the Dublin *Daily Express* newspaper, in which Joyce's first journalism appeared as book reviews, and he donated St Stephen's Green to all the people of Dublin, including the schoolboy James Joyce, who later wrote of his alter ego, Stephen Dedalus, in *A Portrait of the Artist as a Young Man*: 'Crossing Stephen's, that is, my green.'

The Guinness brothers appear first in Episode 5, where Bloom imagines that 'Lord Ardilaun has to change his shirt four times a day' (a claim that seems to have had no basis in fact). Bloom then tries to calculate how many pints of porter (Guinness) would need to be sold to produce a profit of a million pounds to cover the 'sevenfigure cheque for a million' that Ardilaun's brother, Lord Iveagh, once reputedly cashed in the Bank of Ireland. The appearance of the Guinness brothers in this episode – called 'Lotus Eaters', after the drugging of the shipmates of Homer's Ulysses by lotus flower leaves – is an unmistakable allusion to alcohol being the chief narcotic of Dubliners in 1904.

'A million pounds,' muses Bloom, whose contradistinction from almost everyone else in this episode is established in the very first sentence where he walks 'soberly' along Sir John Rogerson's Quay. He continues:

wait a moment. Twopence a pint, fourpence a quart, sixpence a gallon of porter, no, one and fourpence a gallon of porter.

One and four into twenty: fifteen about. Yes, exactly. Fifteen million of barrels of porter. What am I saying barrels? Gallons. About a million barrels all the same.

While Bloom is musing thus under a railway bridge, a train passes overhead and he imagines it to be carrying coaches full of barrels of Guinness that leak out in a huge dull flood 'flowing together, winding through mudflats all over the level land, a lazy pooling swirl of liquor bearing along wideleaved flowers of its froth'.

The Guinness brothers are also referred to in the 'Cyclops' episode, which is set in Barney Kiernan's pub on Little Britain Street, off Capel Street, where the barman, Terence O'Ryan, serves a customer 'a crystal cup full of the foaming ebon ale which the noble twin brothers Bungiveagh and Bungardilaun brew ever in their divine alevats, cunning as the sons of deathless Leda'. The narrator adds that the brothers (who were not twins) 'garner the succulent berries of the hop and mass and sift and bruise and brew them and they mix therewith sour juices and bring the must to the sacred fire and cease not night or day from their toil, those cunning brothers, lords of the vat'. ('The brewery of Messrs Arthur Guinness, Son and Company (Limited)' is also one of the scenes depicted on the Citizen's handkerchief.)

Later, in the 'Circe' episode, set in and around a north inner-city brothel, Bello talks of washing down a good breakfast with 'a bottle of Guinness's porter' and mentions that 'bythebye Guinness's preference shares are at sixteen three quarters'.[18]

'Circe' also features the reappearance of the Galway priest whose schoolroom beating of the young James Joyce is retold graphically in *A Portrait of the Artist as a Young Man*. This is Fr James Daly from Ahascragh, whose presence in the brothel is signalled when 'the bald little round jack-in-the-box head of Father Dolan springs up'. Under his fictional name, Father Dolan, the cruel teacher based on Father Daly is challenged by a version of the benign Jesuit Father John Conmee, who taught and championed the schoolboy James Joyce. 'Any boy want flogging?' asks 'Father Dolan' in a near word-for-word repetition of what 'Baldyhead Dolan' said in *A Portrait of the Artist as a Young Man*: 'Broke his glasses? Lazy little schemer. See it in your eye.'

Before Stephen can reply, 'Don John Conmee' intervenes. Conmee, who is 'Mild, benign, rectorial, reproving', says: 'Now, Father Dolan! Now. I'm sure that Stephen is a very good little boy.'

The Galway-born journalist and author Frank Harris is praised by one of the librarians in the National Library, who says that 'his articles on Shakespeare in the *Saturday Review* were surely brilliant'.[19] Harris was born on Sea Road when his father was serving in the British navy and he spent some of his teenage years in Galway when his elder brother, Vernon, was attending University College Galway. Harris' writings on Shakespeare are also mentioned in the note on 'The Dark Lady of the Sonnets' in the programme notes Joyce wrote for the English Players performances in Zurich in 1918, at the same time as Nora appeared in *Riders to the Sea*.

The MP David Sheehy, who is referred to twice, represented South Galway in the House of Commons in London from 1885 to 1900. He was the father of Richard J. Sheehy, who became Professor of Law at UCG from 1913 to 1923, and the great-grandfather of Dr Micheline Sheehy-Skeffington, who won a landmark gender discrimination case against NUIG at the State's Employment Appeals Tribunal in 2014. The Sheehys were neighbours of the Joyces for a few years and James and his brother Stanislaus were often invited to soirées at the Sheehy home near Mountjoy Square during their teenage years and later.[20]

'House of Horne', 'Horne's House' and 'Horne's Hall' are the names Joyce gave the National Maternity Hospital, Holles Street, where the joint master in 1904 was Dr Andrew Horne, a native of Ballinasloe, and where an entire episode of Ulysses in set.

In addition to real Galwegians a famous fictional one is also namechecked. 'What had Gretta Conroy on?' Leopold Bloom asks early in the morning, referring to the Galway woman who is the heroine of 'The Dead'. Gretta Conroy is one of a number of characters from *Dubliners* who reappear in *Ulysses* and Joyce puts her into the thoughts of Bloom when Bloom is musing about writing a story and submitting it to the magazine *Titbits*. He cites 'What had Gretta Conroy on?' as the type of random questions Molly is wont to ask him while they are getting ready in the morning.

Another fictional Galwegian is 'the man for Galway' who appears on a list of 'Irish heroes and heroines of antiquity'. He is presumably taken from a nineteenth-century song whose chorus said 'with debts galore and fun far more, oh that the man for Galway'. The Mayor of Galway is also mentioned, as is 'Waddler Healy', a probable reference to John Healy, a nineteenth-century Archbishop of Tuam. St Jarlath of Tuam is included on a lengthy list of saints and martyrs. Connacht is referred to as 'Connacht the just'. A bowling green is mentioned once, but only in the context of a game of bowls, not the Barnacle family neighbourhood.

Galway is also likely to have been the provenance of the story of the evening Cissy Caffrey 'dressed up in her father's suit and hat and the burned cork moustache and walked down Tritonville Road, smoking a cigarette', near Sandymount strand. Nora Barnacle's friend Mary O'Halloran confirmed to biographer Richard Ellmann that she and Nora used to dress up in men's clothes and ramble around the streets of Galway for fun at a time when young girls were not allowed out at night.

Toft's Amusements, mentioned three times in the 'Circe' episode, were an annual fixture for decades in Eyre Square in Galway city, a stone's throw from Nora Barnacle's childhood homes in Whitehall and Bowling Green.[21] Toft's first came to Galway in 1883, the year before Nora was born, and their fairground attractions filled Eyre Square every summer around Race Week until the 1960s. With their 'hobbyhorse riders from gilded snakes' and 'cumbersome whirligig', Toft's would have been more a feature of Nora's childhood than of Joyce's and she would almost certainly have brought him and their children to the amusements in Eyre Square during the family's Galway visit of 1912. Kitty's cry in *Ulysses* – 'The gas we had on Toft's hobbyhorses. I'm giddy still' – could just as easily have come from the lips of Nora or her children.

Also mentioned in the 'Circe' episode are 'Peggy Griffin', a real Galway name, and 'Lord Mayor Harrington', a namecheck for Timothy Harrington who was the first person to challenge credibly the conviction of Myles Joyce for the Maamtrasna murders and who, as Lord Mayor of Dublin, wrote a reference for James Joyce when he first went to Paris.

Two old Galway customs that are mentioned more than once are likely to have been heard by Joyce from Nora and her uncle, Michael Healy. One was 'passing around the hat' to collect money for the widow and children of someone who died young; the other was carrying a raw potato in one's pocket to ward off rheumatism.

Michael Healy was probably the first person in Galway to receive a copy of *Ulysses*. Joyce told his friend Constantine Curran that Healy had 'all the first editions of all my books up in an attic (probably he never read them) and a great number of my letters'.[22] The books and other materials are likely to have been inherited by Nora's sister, Kathleen Barnacle, via her mother, after Michael Healy's death.

Joyce's other Galway in-laws – the Monaghans in Oughterard – would have ignored or condemned *Ulysses*, according to Ken Monaghan, the nephew who lived longest. Ken Monaghan's mother, May, one of Joyce's young sisters, married a Galway man, Jack Monaghan, in 1918 and she lived with him in Oughterard until his premature death ten years later. Ken Monaghan said that his mother never owned a copy of *Ulysses*, but she did own and read copies of *Dubliners* and *A Portrait of the Artist as a Young Man*. He recalled:

> She was conscious of his reputation in Ireland and would say to my two sisters and myself that while we should never deny that we were related to Joyce, we did not have to advertise the fact either. James Joyce was not a subject that came up for much discussion at the Monaghan tea table.

He also said that at Jack Monaghan's mother's funeral, one of her sisters is reputed to have declared: 'Isn't it the mercy of God that our dear sister died without knowing that her beloved son was married to the sister of that Antichrist, James Joyce.'[23]

A worse fate befell an early edition of *Ulysses* that Joyce and Nora sent to Frank O'Gorman of O'Gorman's bookshop and printing works on Shop Street (now Eason's), where Nora's sister Kathleen worked in the book bindery and where Nora herself may have also been employed as a temporary casual worker in her teenage years. The book was inscribed 'To Frank, with best wishes, Nora and Jim' – but it did not survive for long in Galway. 'I'm afraid my good Catholic grandmother burnt the copy of *Ulysses*,' Frank O'Gorman's son Ronnie recalled. 'My father was working in the bookselling part of the business and I suppose Nora was hoping he'd buy copies to help sales. This was before the brouhaha made the handling of the book toxic. It was then that Granny O'Gorman burnt the dreadful book,' he added.[24]

Toxic or not, *Ulysses* is not mentioned in the lists of books stocked in Galway's public libraries for several decades after its publication, and the extant minutes of the Galway County Council Libraries Committee indicate that it was extremely unlikely to have been purchased by the committee during the decades when it was tacitly banned in Ireland. The first general meeting of the Galway County Council Libraries Committee – the new State's successor to the County Galway Carnegie Libraries – was held in May 1926, a little over four years after the publication of *Ulysses*. The meeting approved a report from the chief librarian which said:

No little difficulty has been experienced in book selection, particularly in dealing with works of fiction as the general tendency in recent years of authors has lain more in the realm of sex, psycho-analysis, and other objectionable studies totally extraneous to any story.[25]

The librarian's complaint may have been a deliberate or an unintended synopsis of *Ulysses*, but the report went on to say that 'every effort has been made by the committee to ensure that no books of an objectionable nature should be allowed to circulate' and that where a complaint (however trivial) was received relative to any book, such work had been withdrawn at once.

The report also said that the committee was 'an educational institution' whose aim for readers was 'self-development in an atmosphere of freedom', but the first meeting also agreed that 'the authority of the committee be received for the purchase of any book or books and ... that a copy of all books suggested for purchase be sent to the Archbishop of Tuam'. Within a year, in February 1927, the committee also resolved that copies of all books recommended for purchase be supplied 'to each member of the committee, the Archbishop of Tuam, and the Bishop of Galway'. Two months later the two bishops were invited to submit lists of books for purchase and in the following year the committee resolved 'that the books objected to, and at present reserved, be destroyed'.[26]

Galway readers continued to be denied access to *Ulysses*, except clandestinely, after a United States court had ruled in 1933 that the book was not obscene and after it became freely available in England in 1936.[27] In February 1940 – the last year of James Joyce's life – the Galway County Libraries Committee agreed to include on the agenda of its next meeting a motion proposed by long-serving member Professor Liam O Buachalla – a Fianna Fáil senator and University College Galway economics lecturer – 'that excepting books of a technical nature (viz. those relating to agriculture and other industries) no books be purchased in the next twelve months unless printed and published in Eire'.[28]

A decade later, after Joyce and Nora had died, the minutes of the Galway County Libraries Committee's annual meeting noted: 'It was proposed by County Councillor Tom King (Corrandulla), seconded by Tadg O'Shea (Rossaveel), and resolved that printed slips be inserted in every book issued at headquarters, branches and centres, asking readers to draw the attention of the County Librarian to any objectionable book' and that lists of books for purchase be submitted to the Book Selection Sub-Committee (which always included a number of Catholic priests).[29]

The library of the National University of Ireland Galway (formerly University College Galway and originally Queen's College Galway) contains a first edition of *Ulysses*, but neither it nor any other Joyce work appears on the English department's prescribed texts for students until almost a half a century after its publication, and nearly thirty years after Joyce's death.

Students in the 1920s and 1930s were instead required to read, for instance, *The Masters of English Literature* by Stephen Gwynn, the revised 1931 edition of which mentioned some 228 writers but not James Joyce.[30] In the 1940s and 1950s Joyce and his works were still shunned at UCG, despite the publication of a growing number of biographies and studies and the awakening of interest in him, particularly in universities in the United States.

Even the arrival at UCG of Oxford University Professor of English (and author of *The Hobbit* and *The Lord of the Rings*) J.R.R. Tolkien, as an external examiner made no difference.[31] Jointly with UCG's Professor of English Language and English Literature between 1934 and 1965, Jeremiah Murphy, Tolkien set the BA Degree honours and pass examination papers in the late 1940s and 1950s. Their BA Degree honours paper in autumn 1950 – almost a decade after Joyce's death and shortly before Nora's – overlooked Molly Bloom and her creator in asking the undergraduates to 'Discuss the part played by the principal female characters ... in the novels of Jane Austin, Charles Dickens, W.M. Thackeray, Emily Brontë and Thomas Hardy'.

The first mention of Joyce on the college curriculum was in the academic year 1967–8, when Lorna Reynolds was appointed Professor of Modern English following the retirement of Professor Murphy.[32] Joyce was still not recommended for First Arts students, but T.S. Eliot's *James Joyce: Selected Writings*, a Faber & Faber paperback, appeared at the bottom of the list of prescribed texts for BA degree students in that year.[33]

Two years later BA degree students were asked for the first time to answer questions on Joyce, with a choice of two questions on both the 1969 summer and autumn examination papers (although one of the autumn questions was spoiled by the insertion of an erroneous apostrophe in the *Finnegans Wake* title).[34]

UCG's archives appear to contain no record of when the first edition of *Ulysses* was acquired or donated. 'There is certainly no mention of it in the Governing Body minutes or in any correspondence,' says chief archivist Kieran Hoare. 'It is with copies of *Exiles* and *A Portrait of the Artist as a Young Man* which look like they were bound in the 1960s/70s, although *Ulysses* itself is certainly a first edition,' he adds.[35]

Galway's biggest bookshop in the middle and third quarter of the twentieth century, Kennys on High Street, did sell *Ulysses*, although demand was not great in those decades according to Tom Kenny, one of five of the six children of the founders, Des and Maureen, who still work in the business. 'I have only vague memories of copies of *Ulysses* in the shop,' he said. 'As a second-hand bookshop we never had many copies and I am fairly sure they were sold openly.'[36]

Kennys Bookshop was established in 1940 and it published the first biography of Nora Barnacle in June 1982 at a time when the shop had already attracted many distinguished visitors associated with Joyce. 'I remember Sylvia Beach having a long chat with my mother and I remember Richard Ellmann coming to the shop [around the time that] he bought the Joyce collection that Kathleen Barnacle had,' said Tom Kenny.[37]

Before Richard Ellmann came to Galway, Kathleen and her husband, Jack Griffin, a French Polisher from Galway city, had offered to sell some Joyce manuscripts to a Galway city businessman. 'What would I want them for?' he replied.[38]

Joyce told Michael Healy in 1935 that his works 'ought to be worth much more as years go by'[39] and the price of first editions or signed copies rose steadily in the decades after his death. A first edition of *Ulysses* was sold for €409,840 – a world record for a twentieth-century first edition – at Christie's in New York in 2002 and another first edition fetched €315,000 in 2009. A first edition of *Dubliners* was sold at Christie's in New York for €221,450 in 2002. 'For collectors, a copy of the 1914 first edition of *Dubliners* – originally priced at three shillings and sixpence – is one of the most sought-after books of the 20th century,' according to the *Irish Times* auction rooms reporter Michael Parsons.[40]

Copies of *Ulysses* purchased in France, where it was first printed and published, are also valuable. Tom Kenny possesses one rare copy with an unexpected signature. 'I have a two-volume paperback set of *Ulysses*, published in France,' he said. 'Each volume carries the signature "Michael+Galway", so Bishop Browne was a covert Joycean after all!' he said. 'It was a surprise some years ago', he added, 'when we bought an elderly local priest's library to discover a two-volume paperback set of *Ulysses* by James Joyce which was published by the Odyssey Press. This was the ultimate 'dirty book'; 500 copies of the 2nd printing were burned by New York Post Office; 499 copies of the 500 numbered copies in the 3rd printing were seized by Customs Authorities in Folkstone, and yet here it was in a Galway Parish Priest's Library. We got an even bigger shock when we opened the flyleaf and discovered the signature '+M. Browne 1938'. Cross Michael himself, the Bishop!'[41]

Ulysses was not published in Britain until fourteen years after its first publication in Paris. When it was published in England in 1936, Joyce wrote to Mrs Annie Barnacle from Paris to thank her and her daughter Kathleen 'for your message of congratulations on the publication of *Ulysses* in England after my twenty years' struggle'.

He added: 'It is, I may add, the only word of congratulations which has reached me from any Irishman or woman at home or abroad.'[42]

5

BUCK

'Dr O.S. Jesus Gogarty'

Our worthy acquaintance, Mr Malachi Mulligan
— *Ulysses* (14:585)

... the primrose elegance and townbred manners of Malachi
Roland St John Mulligan
— *Ulysses* (14:1,093)

That Mulligan is a contaminated bloody doubledyed ruffian by
all accounts. His name stinks all over Dublin.
— Simon Dedalus in *Ulysses* (6:57)

DOCTOR OLIVER ST JOHN GOGARTY – Malachi or Buck Mulligan in
Ulysses – had a short but intense friendship with Joyce between 1901
and 1904 when they were students and near-neighbours in Dublin's
north inner city. They briefly and famously shared accommodation in
the Martello Tower in Sandycove, south Dublin, where the first episode of *Ulysses* is set.

Gogarty later became the owner of Renvyle House, near Clifden,
between 1917 and 1952. He also owned Dunguaire Castle in Kinvara
for more than thirty years. A surgeon and writer, he spent much of
each year in Galway and he composed sentimental poems about
Galway city, Oughterard, Connemara and the Dublin–Galway train.

Less than a year after the first publication of his poem 'Galway', Renvyle House was burned to the ground by the IRA in February 1923 because of Gogarty's support for the Anglo-Irish Treaty and his membership of the first Free State Senate. A founder of the original Sinn Féin party, he was also abducted in Dublin by IRA gunmen during the Civil War and he swam across the Liffey to escape. He set aside a bedroom and bathroom in his Dublin house for Michael Collins and a key to that house was found in Collins' pocket when he was killed at Béal na Bláth. He also paid the master sculptor Albert Power – whose Pádraic Ó Conaire statue in Eyre Square was a Galway landmark for most of the twentieth century – to travel to London to sculpt the death mask of Terence McSwiney, the Lord Mayor of Cork who died after a seventy-five-day hunger strike in Brixton jail in London in 1920.

Letters from Joyce to Gogarty were among the items lost in the Renvyle House fire, which destroyed everything except the chimney stacks.[1] Gogarty recalled:

In that house was lost my mother's self-portrait, painted when she was a girl of sixteen. Her first attempt in oils. And her sampler of the big parrot, made with thousands of beads, outcome of patience and peaceful days half a hundred years ago, under the tuition of the nuns of Taylor's Hill ... Books, pictures, all consumed: for what? Nothing left but a charred oak beam quenched in the well beneath the house. And ten tall square towers, chimneys, stand bare on Europe's extreme verge.[2]

Gogarty rebuilt Renvyle House in 1928 and he opened it as a hotel in 1930. 'My house stands ... in the faery land of Connemara at the extreme end of Europe ... the world's end,' he wrote in his 1936 memoir *As I Was Going Down Sackville Street*, a title he took from an eighteenth-century Dublin street ballad whose rediscovery he attributed to James Joyce. The memoir's opening pages are devoted to the perambulations of a Dublin eccentric, Endymion or James Boyle Tisdell Burke Stewart Fitzsimmons Farrell, who also makes several fleeting appearances in *Ulysses*. As Malachi Mulligan, the young Gogarty is prominent in several episodes of *Ulysses* in which Joyce also allows him to recite three verses of his poem 'The Song of the Cheerful (but slightly sarcastic) Jazus', retitled 'The Ballad of Joking Jesus' by Joyce.[3]

Gogarty was born in a four-storey, over-basement Georgian house on Rutland Square (now Parnell Square and then 'the grandest of all the Dublin squares', as he described it), opposite the Rotunda Hospital and the Gate Theatre, and he spent childhood summers in Salthill. His mother was Margaret Oliver, from a Galway milling family with a house on Eyre Square. She was educated by the Dominican nuns in Taylor's Hill, and she was, according to Gogarty's contemporary Padraic Colum, a wealthy snob. Colum recalled: 'She was a Miss Oliver of Galway. Like all Galway people she was very "conscious"; she was inclined to look down on people who did not live in one of the squares of Dublin that still had a suggestion of aristocracy.'[4]

Gogarty was four years older than Joyce and their brief friendship cooled before Joyce left Dublin with Nora Barnacle and Gogarty qualified as a medical doctor. Joyce first criticised Gogarty in print in his satirical poem 'The Holy Office', written in the summer of 1904, as 'him whose conduct "seems to own" his preference for a man of tone'. The 'man of tone' was Gogarty's English friend, Samuel Trench, who appears as Haines in the opening episode of *Ulysses*. 'Forgotten friendship?' muses Stephen in the same episode when he feels he's being patronised by Mulligan. Joyce suggested to his brother Stanislaus that he partly based the boastful journalist Ignatius Gallaher in the *Dubliners* short story 'A Little Cloud' on Gogarty and in a letter to Stanislaus he referred to him as 'Dr O.S. Jesus Gogarty'.[5] He also mentions him by name in *Giacomo Joyce*. When Joyce left Dublin with Nora shortly after the publication of 'The Holy Office' and the row in the Martello Tower in Sandymount, Gogarty wrote to a friend that Joyce had fled Dublin and that 'a slavey shared his flight'.[6]

Joyce claimed that Gogarty told him after their relationship cooled that he didn't 'care a damn what you say of me so long as it is literature',[7] but Gogarty later condemned Joyce's habit of surreptitiously recording events and sayings for use in his fictions: 'Secrecy of any kind corrupts sincere relations. I don't mind being reported, but to be an unwilling contributor to one of his "Epiphanies" is irritating.'[8]

Nearly ten years after Joyce's death, Gogarty wrote that he was bemused by the burgeoning interest in Joyce studies among American academics. 'America hailed this Babel from the Berlitz schools of Europe,' he said in reference to *Finnegans Wake*. He also told a Dublin friend: 'You and I would be anathema to the authorities on Joyce, because we knew him,' adding: 'An investigator would be shocked to realize from our talk how little of a prophet Joyce appears to his own countrymen.'[9]

The enmity that grew between Joyce and Gogarty is expressed most fiercely in *Ulysses*, where Stephen Dedalus' father, Simon, calls Malachi Mulligan a 'cad' and goes on:

> That Mulligan is a contaminated bloody doubledyed ruffian by all accounts. His name stinks all over Dublin. But with the help of God and His blessed mother I'll make it my business to write a letter one of those days to his mother or his aunt or whoever she is that will open her eye as wide as a gate. I'll tickle his catastrophe, believe you me ... I won't have her bastard of a nephew ruin my son. A counterjumper's son.

The aunt to whom Simon Dedalus is referring is modelled on Annie Oliver, an unmarried sister of Gogarty's mother who lived in the Rutland Square house during Oliver's childhood and teenage years. Born in Galway in 1849, she would have been aged about fifty when her nephew became friendly with Joyce, who mentions her three times in the opening episode of *Ulysses* and twice in two other early episodes, underlining her influence on Gogarty. 'The aunt thinks you killed your mother,' Buck Mulligan tells Stephen in one of their opening exchanges, adding: 'That's why she won't let me have anything to do with you.'

Evidence that Gogarty's mother and aunt banned Joyce from their house after they learned that he had declined to pray at his dying mother's bedside has been unearthed among the papers of Joyce and Gogarty's contemporaries.[10] In a letter to Tom Kettle, a student friend of the two men who later became a Nationalist MP and a poet before being killed in the First World War, Mrs Gogarty wrote:

> I have been wishing for an opportunity of speaking to you about Oliver for a long time. You can do him an inestimable service by your companionship and advice to counteract the evil effects of others, one, especially, a bad Catholic who spent a great deal of time with Oliver last winter before I discovered he was, or pretended to be, an Agnostic, so I forbade him to call here any more.

In another letter two days later, Mrs Gogarty told Kettle:

> If I could only speak to you for a short time you would much better understand the need there is to counteract the influences to which he is subjected.

Joyce's irreligiousity was not the only reason for his being shunned by Gogarty's mother and aunt. Mulligan's next remark in *Ulysses* – 'The aunt always keeps plain-looking servants for Malachi. Lead him not into temptation' – is a reminder that the Gogarty household employed two servants at the time when Joyce's family, which had servants when James was a young boy, had now become impecunious. Later, Mulligan teases Stephen by warning him: 'The aunt is going to call on your unsubstantial father.'

The deteriorating relationship between the two friends can be traced through the succeeding episodes of *Ulysses* – Mulligan is mentioned in ten of the eighteen. 'Hast thou found me, O mine enemy?' Stephen asks himself silently when Mulligan bursts into the group that Stephen is addressing in the National Library, after Stephen had failed to keep an appointment to join Mulligan for a drinking session. Successive subsequent references are increasingly sarcastic: 'young Mulligan'; 'Mal. Mulligan a gentleman's gentleman'; 'Our worthy acquaintance, Mr Malachi Mulligan'; 'the primrose elegance and townbred manners of Malachi Roland St John Mulligan'; 'Dr Malachi Mulligan, sex specialist'; 'Mercurial Malachi' and 'Father Malachi O'Flynn' whose intoning of *Introibo ad altare diaboli* echoes Mulligan's *Introibo ad altare Dei* on the novel's opening page.

The final references to the fractured friendship are left to Leopold Bloom, who has observed Stephen and Mulligan in the National Library and the National Maternity Hospital and who has seen Mulligan 'give Stephen the slip' at Westland Row station when he did not want to bring him back to the tower in Sandycove. Having rescued the inebriated Stephen from a row with two British soldiers, Bloom takes him to a nearby cabman's night shelter for coffee and while there he advises him:

> I wouldn't personally repose much trust in that boon companion of yours who contributes the humorous element, Dr Mulligan, as a guide, philosopher, and friend, if I were in your shoes. He knows which side his bread is buttered on though in all probability he never realized what it is to be without regular meals. Of course you didn't notice as much as I did but it wouldn't occasion me the least surprise to learn that a pinch of tobacco or some narcotic was put in your drink for some ulterior object.

And Joyce's valedictory verdict in the novel on his former pal is Bloom's silent summer 1904 reflection on Mulligan, written a decade and a half later:

> He understood, however, from all he heard, that Dr Mulligan was a versatile allround man, by no means confined to medicine only, who was rapidly coming to the fore in his line

and, if the report was verified, bade fair to enjoy a flourishing practice in the not too distant future as a tony medical practitioner drawing a handsome fee for his services in addition to which professional status his rescue of that man from certain drowning by artificial respiration and what they call first aid at Skerries, or Malahide was it? was, he was bound to admit, an exceedingly plucky deed which he could not too highly praise, so that frankly he was utterly at a loss to fathom what earthly reason could be at the back of it except he put it down to sheer cussedness or jealousy, pure and simple.

Gogarty, who had saved a man from drowning in the Liffey, and who is also likely to be the 'eye, ear, nose and throat witness' from 'Medical Square' who appears in *Finnegans Wake*,[11] written another decade later, hit back viciously, although his most caustic criticism only appeared in print outside Ireland and not until nearly ten years after Joyce's death.[12]

Increasingly irritated in later life that his own artistic and medical achievements were being overshadowed by his portrayal as Buck Mulligan in *Ulysses*, Gogarty wrote that Joyce was 'the most predamned soul I have ever encountered' and he described *Ulysses* as 'a triumph of ugliness and chaos and ineffectuality', a 'stink bomb for Dublin' and 'one of the most depressing things that has come out of literature'.

In a lead article in the *Saturday Review of Literature*, a New York weekly, Gogarty wrote that he found amusement 'here and there' in *Ulysses*, but he condemned it as a 'cracked mirror ... with its preposterous and factitious parallel to Homer's fairy tale'.[13] He added:

I wonder what all the worshippers of Joyce would say if they realized that they had become the victims of a gigantic hoax, one of the most enormous leg-pulls in history. ... When we think of anyone hailing *Ulysses* and *Finnegans Wake* as all the world's erudition in disguise, the question of the sanity, or even of the literacy, of the Joyce enthusiast arises.[14]

Gogarty wrote the *Saturday Review of Literature* piece – in the St Patrick's Weekend edition in 1950 – after he had read an academic analysis of the 'Oxen of the Sun' episode in *Ulysses*, which is set in the National Maternity Hospital in Holles Street and in which Buck Mulligan features prominently. 'That's what we've come to,' he told a friend in New York. '[Joyce] once spent an evening with me in Holles Street Hospital. And now some character in Canada is probably getting a Ph.D. for analyzing his profound knowledge of midwifery.'[15]

Joyce, in contrast to his former friend, had mellowed after *Ulysses* was published, and when he died one of the two books found on his desk was Gogarty's recently published *I Follow Saint Patrick*. Less than a month before he died, Joyce mentioned Gogarty when he met the Irish diplomat Seán Lester in Geneva. 'He spoke of Oliver Gogarty about whom he enquired and about his hotel in the West,' Lester recorded in his diary.[16]

Joyce had also shown that he was pleased when Gogarty escaped uninjured from an aeroplane mishap in Connemara in 1928. In that incident, which Joyce read about in a *Connacht Tribune* probably sent to him by Annie Barnacle, Gogarty and his pilot, Lady Mary Elliot Heath, had to be rescued by local fishermen when their aircraft landed on quicksand on Tallaghbawn Strand, near Muilrea. 'Immediately the plane began to sink and Dr Oliver nobly said to me "You jump out and get clear first",' Lady Heath told a reporter from the *Connacht Tribune*. She said that the landing was 'a pretty thrilling moment', but the aircraft was only dragged clear of the quicksand after strenuous efforts by the fishermen using ropes.[17]

The *Connacht Tribune* report was headlined 'Fishermen to the Rescue' and it was accompanied by two photographs of Lady Heath, taken in the South Park in the Claddagh when she landed there a week earlier. After Annie Barnacle wrote to Joyce about the report he promptly sent a humorous account of the incident to Harriet Weaver, before adding that he was glad that Gogarty and his pilot were both uninjured.[18]

Gogarty had been captivated by Connemara after he married Martha Duane, from Moyard, near Renvyle, in 1906. 'Many-coloured Connemara,' he wrote nearly fifty years later. 'To name them in a language that has hardly a dozen names for colour would be impossible.' He added: 'Were it not for the clouds off the Atlantic that break in rain, I would never leave Renvyle with its glimmering islands and its assured faith in wonders of the deep.'[19]

Travelling to and from Renvyle often involved overnight stays in Galway. 'What a town Galway is,' he wrote, 'beside its rippling, abundant river, swan-laden, salmon-full! ... why should anyone want to go further than Galway? Why indeed?' At the same time, approaching his seventieth birthday, he wrote: 'All my wishes are fulfilled; but if I had one more wish it would be that I might be mayor of Galway even for one year – Galway, a cleaner Venice, with living water in place of brackish, stagnant canals!'[20]

Gogarty's family continued to run Renvyle House as a hotel until they sold it in 1952. Gogarty also reroofed Dunguaire Castle; he entertained W. B. Yeats and Lady Gregory there, but he never completed the renovations.[21] Gogarty hoped that royalties from *As I Was Going Down Sackville Street* would help to pay for the renovations, but instead he was successfully sued for libel over a reference in the book to a Dublin antiques dealer and also ordered to pay all the High Court costs. He spent much of the next twenty years in the United States writing and lecturing. He planned to return to Ireland but he died in New York in 1957. His remains were flown to Shannon Airport before being taken by road to Connemara (passing through Oranmore village, where one of his aunts, Mother Joseph Oliver, had been one of the four nuns from Galway who had established the Presentation Convent there nearly a century earlier in 1861, and where his friend Anita Leslie had bought and restored 'the strong castle of Oranmore, the fortress that guarded the approach by "the Great Shore" to Galway from the South'[22]). He is buried with his wife and maternal grandmother in Ballinakill cemetery, near Renvyle.

Among the verses in his poem 'Connemara' are:

There's something sleeping in my breast
That wakens only in the West;
There's something in the core of me
That needs the West to set it free.

And I can see that river flow
Beside the town of Ballinasloe
To bound a country that is worth
The half of Heaven, the whole of Earth.

And:

As often as I take the road
Beyond the Suck, I wish to God
That it were but a one-way track
Which I might take and not come back.

The refrain of his poem 'Galway' is:

Take in my heart your place again
Between your lake and sea,
O city of the watery plain
You mean so much to me.

6

ROCK

'When the Galway harbour scheme was mooted'

Ask her captain, he advised them, how much palmoil the
British Government gave him for that day's work.
    — *Ulysses* (16:876)

We shall find that Liverpool gold was brought to bear on the
transaction.
    — *Galway Vindicator and Connaught Advertiser*, Wednesday, 23
    June 1858

THE GROUNDING OF THE PASSENGER STEAMSHIP *Indian Empire* on the
Margaretta Rock in Galway Bay on 16 June 1858, which is referred to
twice in *Ulysses*, was certainly suspicious.[1] Rumours about the incident
lingered in Galway, where efforts to establish the harbour as a major
transatlantic gateway continued for decades despite competition from
much larger ports in Liverpool, Southampton and northern Europe.

Joyce undoubtedly heard the story from Nora or her relatives,
among whom it would have been common currency in what was still
the small port city of Galway. Nora's maternal uncle, Michael Healy,
who maintained a lifelong friendship with Joyce, would have been
familiar with the details from his many years as Inspector of Customs
and Receiver of Wrecks in Galway.[2]

Michael Healy is also likely to have shown Joyce the Galway Harbour Commissioners' plans to build a new transatlantic port in the

deep water west of Mutton Island to provide the shortest crossing between Europe and the US and Canada. Joyce's empathy for the Galway plan, which re-emerges in *Ulysses*, was evident in one of the articles he wrote from Galway for *Ill Piccolo della Sera* in 1912. 'A large proportion of the goods and passengers which are now landed at Liverpool would in the future come to Galway and proceed directly to London, via Dublin and Holyhead,' he wrote, interpreting the prospectus. 'The old decaying city would rise once again. Wealth and vital energy would flow from the new world through this new artery into blood-drained Ireland.'[3]

Joyce would have found reports of the grounding of the *Indian Empire* in back issues of the *Freeman's Journal*, the daily newspaper whose offices (just off O'Connell Street beside the GPO) he visited and in which he set an entire episode of *Ulysses*. Anniversaries and coincidences were very important to him and the serendipity of the date of the grounding – the date that would come to be known as Bloomsday, thanks to his writing – would have piqued his interest and secured its inclusion in *Ulysses*.

Galway Bay was calm and clear on the near-midsummer night of Tuesday, 15 June, when the *Indian Empire* arrived off the Aran Islands, at the mouth of the bay, where two outer-bay pilots went on board shortly before midnight.[4] With eighty-six hands on board, the 245 foot x 40 foot wooden-hulled steamship was more than two thirds the length of a modern international soccer pitch and was almost certainly the largest vessel to enter the bay up to that night. Built in New York in 1848, it had been chartered to inaugurate a new service from Galway to America, offering passage to New York on its three decks for 19 pounds (first class), 10 pounds (second class) and 7 pounds (steerage). Advertisements in the Galway newspapers said that the 'splendid steamship' would land 'Her Majesty's mails' at Halifax, Nova Scotia, before proceeding to New York. A fireworks display was advertised for Eyre Square (admission sixpence) to celebrate the inaugural sailing, which was scheduled for the following Friday, 18 June. An editorial in the *Galway Mercury* newspaper said that the new service 'proudly professes to join the New World with the Old' and the *Galway Express* editorial announced that 'the authorities have issued a notice stating that all letters for America bearing the words *per Indian Empire* ... will be forwarded from Galway on the same day'.[5]

The two pilots, Henry Burbridge and Patrick Wallace, steered the ship towards Black Head before altering course for Galway harbour. But two and a half hours after they went on board, the ship ran aground 'hard and fast' on the Margaretta Rock on the morning of 16 June, according to the later testimony of the captain, Edwin Courteney.

Captain Courteney immediately retook control of the vessel and refloated it with the help of high tide two and a half hours later. After the ship dropped anchor on the roadstead outside the port, the pilots and crew were brought before an emergency meeting of the Galway Harbour Commissioners. An overflow crowd turned up at the Harbour Commissioners' offices because the grounding had immediately raised suspicions – and a rush to judgment – in Galway and elsewhere.

'Much indignation was expressed at the conduct of the pilots when the occurrence became known here,' reported the *Galway Mercury*, adding: 'the general impression being that it was done through design, and that the pilots were bribed. Wallace was hooted by an excited mob and had to take refuge in the police barracks or he would be roughly handled.'

Elsewhere the same newspaper suggested that the bribes had been paid by 'certain Liverpool interests'. It also carried a report from 'A Dublin Correspondent' which stated:

The excitement and indignation here were extremely great on hearing what had happened to the *Indian Empire* ... it is to be hoped that all those implicated in this foul deed – as a foul deed it is universally represented to be – will be all dragged to light, and made to pay the penalty of their guilt.

Liverpool interests were also blamed by the twice-weekly *Galway Vindicator and Connaught Advertiser*, which stated that the cause of 'this maladorious business shall come out sooner or later and then we shall find that Liverpool gold was brought to bear on the transaction'.[6] It pointed out that 'no blame attaches to the pilots of Galway port' who were responsible only for inner pilotage 'between the quay and Mutton Island',[7] and it also cited a report from the London correspondent of the *Daily Express* that said:

> It is circulated here that money has been freely used by the Liverpool shipping interest and in a manner not to the credit of some persons in particular to frustrate the enterprise of opening up direct steam communication between Galway and the United States.

The *Galway Express* reported that, while it was not yet known whether the grounding happened 'by design or otherwise', the Santa Margaretta rock was large and buoyed 'and so well known that the smallest boy in Claddagh could not mistake it even on the darkest night that ever came from the heavens'. It added:

> When it became known in town what occurred, the indignation of the people was so great that they would have punished them after Lynch law manner if they could have laid hold of the pilots. One of them (Wallace) had to take shelter in the barracks and remain there until he was escorted by the police to the office of the Harbour Commissioners, where there was an investigation going on, whither he was followed by the populace, hooting and groaning him as they went along.

A report dispatched from Galway to the Dublin-based *Freeman's Journal* on the night of the incident said that the grounding 'on a clear and tranquil night' had 'caused a great deal of excitement and much indignation here'. The dispatch, 'From Our Reporter', added: 'There is but one opinion here on the subject, and that is that the thing was done by design; and, indeed, after hearing the facts it is impossible to come to any other conclusion.'

The *Freeman's Journal* – self-described as 'Ireland's national newspaper' and the closest Ireland had to a national daily newspaper in 1858 – devoted more than two full columns on pages two and three to the incident. Its reporter wrote that 'no similar occurrence has taken place within the recollection of any one here', adding: 'Owing to the fortunate circumstance of the captain having, upon his own responsibility, slackened speed, the steamer did not run far upon the rock, and to this is to be attributed her escape with so little an amount of injury.'

A follow-up dispatch to the *Journal* from Galway the next day went further. It said:

> The feeling which prevailed yesterday, that the pilots had intentionally run the *Indian Empire* upon the San Margaretta Rock – the only one in a channel nine miles wide – has now become almost a settled conviction; and from the facts which have been proved, it seems impossible that it should be otherwise. Founded on this conviction that a base attempt was made to defeat a great national project, there is the greatest indignation in the public mind here. Everyone with whom I have spoken on the subject says that such a transaction should put beyond all question, in the minds of every honourable man, not merely in Ireland and America, but also in England, the clear natural right of Galway to a fair trial of her claim to be an American Packet Station, if not to an immediate practical recognition of that claim. Providentially, the alleged design of destroying the steamer – if there were a design – was not accomplished.

The special meeting of the Galway Harbour Commissioners, which began at two o'clock on the afternoon of the grounding, was told that 'a bundle of letters ... some of which were postmarked from

Liverpool' was found during a police search of the houses of the pilots, who attended the meeting 'under the protection of a large body of the constabulary', according to the *Freeman's Journal*. The first commissioner to speak was Fr Peter Daly, a maverick Galway Catholic priest who was a co-founder and a co-director of the Galway Line with John Orrell Lever and also a shareholder in the company that had been established to run the line, having offered to invest £20,000 in it, according to Lever.[8]

Daly, who was parish priest of Rahoon and St Nicholas Church and who was also chairman of the Galway Town Commissioners, called for a full inquiry into the grounding to satisfy the public mind not just in Galway, but also in 'the three kingdoms' and in Europe and America. He said that the *Indian Empire* had been intended to be 'the pioneer of a great project of national importance'. He was cheered when he said it was incumbent to hold a full inquiry for the sake of justice and for Galway harbour's reputation, although he himself was inclined to describe the grounding as something other than an accident.

Fr Daly called for criminal charges to be brought and for sworn testimony to be taken at the Magistrates Court 'into everything connected with this unhappy transaction'. He said it was 'a most unfortunate thing that these pilots ever went on board' and he claimed that the ship could have been brought safely into port by any young sailor – or even by himself, although he was almost blind. He wanted to know why the vessel was put on course for 'the only rock in the bay', a rock 'miles out of the way of any vessel coming through the proper channel'. He pointed out that the bay was 9 miles wide at that point, mostly to a depth of between 13 and 20 fathoms, and that there was 6 miles of deep water between the Margaretta rock and the southern shore. He was cheered again when he said that either one of the pilots who were in charge of the vessel could have pointed to the rock, even in the dark, 'as readily as I could point my finger to the hat that is lying on the table before me'.

Captain Courteney told the meeting that he had 'not the slightest hesitation in saying' that he would have brought the vessel safely from Black Head to her harbour moorings without any pilot on board. He said he had commanded ships of all sizes in some of the most difficult harbours in the world. The *Indian Empire*, he said, had a crew of '84 excellent seamen and as good officers as any vessel need have', and that the ship was 'as good as timber, iron and copper could make her'. He said that as 'an old steamship officer' he had insisted on reducing the ship's speed when he first began to doubt the pilots. Had he not slackened the speed, the ship would now be 'in two halves' on the rock, he claimed. He said that the grounding happened suddenly after he defied the pilot who had told him to keep watch on the starboard side. He said he had shouted when he saw the rock on the port side, only to be told by the pilot that what he saw was not a rock, but a boat. Both pilots, he said, did nothing after the ship hit the rock, except remain on deck talking to each other. 'It appeared to me they took the striking of the vessel as a matter of course,' he added.

The two pilots were questioned briefly by the Harbour Board Chairman and 'it was found necessary to direct the police to keep order' after a number of other ship's officers had followed Captain Courteney in severely criticising them. Burbridge, who was described in the Galway newspapers as 'an Englishman' or 'a Welshman', said that the ship's compass may have been at fault and that the ship was aground before the buoy was seen, but Wallace, 'a Galwayman', contradicted some of the things he said.

The meeting was brought to a close by Mr Anthony O'Flaherty, a Justice of the Peace and Deputy Lieutenant of Galway Borough, who said that enough had been heard to place the two pilots under arrest pending an appearance before the Magistrates Court next morning. He also proposed, successfully, that the pilots should be sacked peremptorily by the commissioners. 'The pilots were sent off to jail guarded by a strong body of police, a precaution that was necessary, for the crowd assembled were greatly excited against the accused,' reported the *Freeman's Journal*. The *Galway Express* recorded similarly: 'The pilots were then sent to jail, escorted by a strong body of police, followed by a large crowd of persons, who seemed greatly excited.'

Galway Courthouse was packed to overflowing next morning when the pilots were brought from jail (situated just across the Salmon Weir Bridge, where Galway Cathedral now stands) to appear at the Petty Sessions. Among the magistrates confronting them in court were two of the Galway Harbour Commissioners: Anthony O'Flaherty (chairman) and Pierce Joyce, the High Sheriff of Galway (and almost certainly the same Pierce Joyce of Mervue, Galway – occupation: 'gentleman' – who was also among the later shareholders in the Galway Line's parent company).

'The Courthouse was very much crowded and great interest and excitement seemed to prevail among all present,' reported the *Galway Vindicator and Connaught Advertiser*. It added:

Indeed such a feeling seemed to pervade all classes through the town ... the Courthouse was filled almost to suffocation and the pressure on the galleries was so great that it was found necessary to send the police to relieve the pressure of the crowd on them.

After a three-hour adjournment sought by the pilots' solicitor, who said he had telegraphed to Dublin for a senior counsel and that he expected him down 'on the first train', the proceedings began after 1 p.m. The case was listed as: 'The Queen (at the prosecution of the Galway Harbour Commissioners on the complaint of Edwin Courteney, commander of the steamship *Indian Empire*) versus Henry Burbridge and Patrick Wallace, pilots.'

The pilots faced one charge:

That the defendants, being licensed pilots in Galway Bay, did willfully and maliciously, and through willful neglect and breach of duty, cause the steamship *Indian Empire* to strike upon the Santa Margaretta Rock in Galway Bay on the morning of the 16th of June 1858 thereby leading to the destruction, or serious damage of said ship and to endanger the lives of those on board.

Opening the prosecution case, solicitor Mr Coll Rochford said that his was a 'very painful duty' on many accounts, not the least of which was that the grounding of the *Indian Empire* 'had nearly nipped in the bud an endeavour to make the town of Galway attain to that powerful commercial position which it ought to occupy'. He said that 'through Providence' the men had been defeated 'in their adominable attempt to ruin a great national project' and to destroy a noble and valuable ship and endanger the lives of those on board. He said that they had ignored the captain's observation that the ship was travelling too fast and that it would now be 'a total wreck' had the captain not insisted on slackening speed.

Mr Rochford said that the water was 'tranquil' and the night was clear and that the Margaretta Rock was 'known to every man in Galway' and was marked clearly and distinctly on every chart of the port. He repeated the claim that the pilots had directed the captain to look for the buoy on the starboard side when it was in fact on the port side. Calling on the bench to commit the men for trial, he said: 'What could any man conclude from these facts but that the men who acted in this manner wanted to destroy the ship?'

Captain Courteney was the first of four prosecution witnesses. He blamed the pilots and said that if he had not reduced the ship's speed after entering the bay she 'would have broken her back and become a total wreck' when she hit the rock. He said: 'My conviction then was and now is that the vessel was struck on purpose and I told the pilots so.' He said he would not have steered the course the pilots did, but would have continued to follow the Admiralty Charts, as he had done without incident since leaving Southampton port, bound for Galway.

The Captain said that pilots take 'sole and absolute command' when they board a ship and that the captain 'might go to bed or lie on a sofa', though he did neither. He said he believed the pilots were perfectly sober, but they greeted any remarks he made with 'a great deal of apathy'. He insisted that he would have seen the buoy on the Margaretta Rock much earlier if the pilot Wallace had not directed him to look over the (opposite) starboard bow with his night glasses.

'The night was perfectly clear and almost as bright as day,' he said.

Courteney testified that the Margaretta Rock was clearly marked on the Admiralty Chart and he said that he would have easily avoided it even if there had not been any buoy on it. He said that the presence of the buoy on the rock would have enabled the most illiterate and least experienced seaman on board to have steered the ship safely to anchorage without any pilot.

Under cross-examination the captain said that he would not be justified in interfering with a pilot's course, but that these pilots had put his ship 'hard and fast upon the rock'. He added:

> When I saw the buoy I think it was too late to guard against danger; there was nothing to prevent the pilots from seeing it; I never, I must say, saw pilots manage a ship so badly as these men did from the time they came on board; when pilots come on board it is their duty to keep a look out.

He also said that when he offered his crewmen £1.00 each to exert themselves to try to refloat the vessel, one of the pilots had said the attempt would be futile.

Second officer John McDonald told the court that he had never seen pilots conduct a vessel so badly. He said that he agreed with everything his captain had testified. He also said that when he saw the buoy he had shouted at the pilot Berbridge 'That's a buoy', but that Berbridge had replied: 'That's impossible, it must be a boat.' He said the night was perfectly clear and visibility was about two miles with the naked eye. He said the *Indian Empire* hit the rock a minute and a half after he had shouted about the buoy. He said he himself had often gone up and down the River Thames where there were plenty of buoys and shoals and 'no mischief had happened'.

The ship's purser, Benjamin Lewis Baysham, said he had overheard the exchange between McDonald and Berbridge. He said nobody could mistake a buoy for a boat on such a clear night, adding: 'The pilots acted with great carelessness and apathy.'

Following similar testimony from the fourth witness, Quartermaster William Medlen, the pilots' solicitor said that they were prepared to offer 'any amount of bail that might be required', but the magistrates unanimously rejected the plea and ordered that the prisoners be returned to jail and sent for trial at the next sittings of the Assizes (Circuit Criminal Courts) in Galway, where they would face transportation if found guilty. The Chairman of the Magistrates, Anthony O'Flaherty, who had earlier stated that the Captain's evidence alone was sufficient to send the men forward for trial, said bail was being refused because 'the prosecution case so convincingly brought home to the minds of the magistrates the guilt of the prisoners'. He added that if the prisoners felt aggrieved, they could apply to the Court of the Queen's Bench for bail.

O'Flaherty's opinion was shared by the crowd in the public gallery. 'The dense crowd which thronged the court seemed highly satisfied with the decision of the magistrates and evinced their feelings with a loud cheer,' reported the *Galway Mercury* and the *Galway Express* identically. 'The prisoners were shortly afterwards remanded to the town prison under escort of a large body of armed police, a great number of whom had to be brought in from the neighbouring constabulary stations, to protect the prisoners from the infuriated violence of the populace,' said the *Galway Vindicator and Connaught Advertiser*.

Despite the case now being *sub judice*, the guilt of the pilots was again assumed on only their third night in custody awaiting trial when Fr Peter Daly addressed some two hundred of Galway's civic and business leaders at a public dinner in honour of John Orell Lever. Daly told the diners that Lever's ships would lie safely at anchor in Galway harbour 'if they had no false pilots to deal with'. In the presence of city magistrates and harbour commissioners Anthony O'Flaherty and Pierce Joyce, both seated at the top table, he also noted that Captain Courteney had given sworn evidence in court that 'an illiterate man would bring a vessel safe into this port'.

John Orrell Lever was more circumspect. He said that no man should suffer prejudice or injustice 'without good cause', but he had to say 'at the same time that there was some undercurrent at work' and he added that he had to thank 'not only the gentlemen of the Harbour Board, but also the gentlemen of the bench for the satisfactory manner in which they had conducted the case'. He said, 'they did not want to injure any poor man', but their objective was to find out the cause of the grounding.

Lever said he would favour offering the pilots a free pardon if they would make a statement to say if anyone had bribed them and, if so, for what motive. He was cheered when he said he would subscribe £200 from his own pocket 'to reward them for making known the truth'. He added that their instigators should be brought to justice, but that nobody should seek to punish 'those who have been made the agents of some detestable villain'. He also said that, on the other hand, he would be glad to accept that the accident had happened because the pilots had never piloted so large a ship before and had confused each other, for everybody knew that 'two cooks spoil the broth'. He said he would be very sorry if the men were punished for a grounding that had occurred 'through ignorance or accident'.

The *Tuam Herald*, published on the morning of the Lever dinner, also cautioned against prejudice, but reflected the local suspicions. Its editorial said:

> Great indignation exists throughout the country against the conduct of the pilots who occasioned the slight accident to the *Indian Empire* on her entry last Wednesday to Galway harbour. Grave suspicions attach to the parties concerned in the matter. Until, however, the transaction is cleared up by rigid inquiry and the production of evidence which inculpate or exculpate them, we forbear any comment. It is not fair to prejudge the cause; it looks very suspicious.

The pilots were granted bail by the Court of Queen's Bench after spending a fortnight in custody. However, one of them, Patrick Wallace, died suddenly while awaiting trial, sparking speculation that he had been poisoned or had taken his own life. 'Mysterious and sudden death of Patrick Wallace, the Pilot', ran the headline on the *Galway Express* on 24 July. Three doctors told a preliminary inquest at the Courthouse that he had died 'from the effects of poison'. One of them, Dr Charles Croker King, a fellow of the Royal College of Surgeons in Ireland, said the body showed no sign of disease and that the death was due to 'no natural cause'.

Wallace's widow, Mary, told the inquest that he was 'always fretting' about the pilotage following his release on bail and she thought that that caused his death. She said he was uneasy about the forthcoming trial and he used to sigh through his sleep at night. She said he had been with the other pilot, Mr Burbridge, on the night before he died, but that he was 'quite well' when he came home at midnight.

Samples taken from Wallace's stomach were sent to police headquarters in Dublin for examination and the inquest was adjourned for ten days; during which time rumours spread. A letter was sent to the authorities in Dublin Castle and to various newspapers stating that Wallace had died from strangulation. Under the headline 'Mysterious Death' the *Galway Mercury* noted 'various rumours of the cause of death having been afloat in the town', while the *Galway Vindicator and Connaught Advertiser* recorded that 'considerable sensation was caused in the town by the report of the sudden death of Patrick Wallace ... from a report that his death had not occurred from natural causes, a great deal of interest was felt in the matter'.

The inquest and criminal proceedings having been adjourned, a high-powered delegation from Galway travelled to London in the first week of August to petition the government for money to develop the harbour so that it could accommodate larger vessels for the nascent transatlantic services. But news of the *Indian Empire* mishap had preceded the members there. 'What sort of passage did the *Indian Empire* make?' was one of the first questions the Prime Minister Lord Derby asked Fr Peter Daly when he received the delegation in Downing Street.

The ensuring exchanges, as recorded by a *Freeman's Journal* correspondent and reported in the *Tuam Herald*, included the following:

> FR DALY: She met with an accident before she started, and after she left another accident happened, which deprived her of a considerable portion of her power.
>
> THE EARL OF DERBY: She ran upon the only rock to be found in the neighbourhood, did she not (a laugh)?'
>
> FR DALY: She was run upon a rock, and the two pilots who had her in charge were committed for trial for the offence. One of them is since dead.
>
> THE EARL OF DERBY: By suicide?
>
> FR DALY: That has not yet been ascertained, as his stomach has not been analysed.

The Prime Minister, who was also First Lord of Her Majesty's Treasury and Leader of the House of Lords, as well as Conservative Party leader, gave no commitment except that the funding request would be considered. Fr Daly, who spoke for the delegation although it also included two Galway MPs, William Gregory and Lord Dunkellin, and the High Sheriff of Galway, as well as Sir John Lever, said that 'the small sum of one hundred and fifty-two thousand pounds' would enable the Harbour Board to build a new breakwater and pier near Mutton Island. He said that his petition was delivered on behalf of the Harbour Commissioners, Town Commissioners 'and inhabitants of Galway'.[9]

The resumed inquest into the death of Patrick Wallace was reported less prominently in the local newspapers. The jury at the Courthouse was now told that analysis of the samples at police headquarters had found no trace of mineral or vegetable poison in Wallace's stomach. Dr Charles Croker King told the jury and the Town and County Coroner, Robert Stephens: 'After the most careful consideration of the case, I have come to the conclusion that death did not arise from poison or from any violence whatsoever.' He added that there was no evidence whatsoever to support the claim in the letter sent to Dublin Castle and the newspapers that death was due to strangulation. The jury returned a verdict that Patrick Wallace had died 'from natural causes and by the visitation of God'.

The trial of the other pilot, Burbridge, appears to have been adjourned indefinitely – no record of it can be found in the Galway Assizes reports in the local newspapers over the next year – and the *Indian Empire* continued to cross the Atlantic between Galway and New York on a regular schedule for some time. Although the damage sustained in the grounding was repaired and the vessel was able to withstand a fierce five-day storm off the Mayo coast in November, earning Captain Courteney high praise from his passengers and crew, her maiden visit to Galway was the first of a series of setbacks that bedevilled the attempts to establish a thriving transatlantic passenger service from there. And the money sought from Her Majesty's Treasury for a new breakwater and pier never materialised, although Fr Daly's deputation 'returned much pleased with their mission', according to the *Tuam Herald*.

The grounding and subsequent trial are not mentioned in the authorised history of the Galway Harbour Commissioners, in which the brief reference to the inaugural transatlantic crossing of the *Indian Empire* also fails to acknowledge that the voyage took a longer-than-expected twelve days because of the damage sustained by one of the vessel's four boilers when it hit the Margaretta Rock.[10] The grounding was reported in *Lloyd's List*, the City of London daily newspaper that recorded ship movements and port activities throughout the British Empire. Its Thursday, 17 June edition carried a report dated Galway, 16 June, which said: 'The INDIAN EMPIRE (s), from Southampton, ran on the St Margaretta Rocks this morning, but got off without any apparent damage, and lies at anchor in this roadstead, without making water.' Two days later the paper reported that the vessel had sailed for Halifax, Nova Scotia, and other ports.

The public dinner in honour of Sir John Orrell Lever on the night before the inaugural sailing was presided over by Fr Peter Daly in

'Mrs Carrigan's Great Rooms' on Eyre Square. The *Freeman's Journal* noted: 'Nearly 200 of the principal proprietors of the county, leading merchants and traders of the town were present, and great enthusiasm in the project was manifested.' The *Galway Express* also reported: 'Immediately behind the chair was a large flag bearing the red cross of England and behind the vice-chair was another large flag bearing the stars and stripes, the emblem of the great republic of America.'

John Orrell Lever told the meeting that the project initiated by the sailing of the *Indian Empire*

> was looked on with interest not only in the United Kingdom and in America, but in France and Germany and other parts of the Continent, for when it was in regular order he believed that such through-traffic arrangements would be made as they would have passengers coming from Hamburg through England to Galway, and carried to America for £7 a head, and that expeditiously, instead of, as at present, losing days in Hull, inquiring about a ship to New York; or, if they went to Liverpool, getting into the hands of crimps, who robbed them.

The first anniversary of the inaugural transatlantic sailing of the *Indian Empire* from Galway was marked by another fireworks display in Eyre Square. Rockets were also fired from the vessel itself and from another ship anchored outside the harbour. The *Galway Mercury* reported that the 'fine display of rockets ... had a grand effect on the bay as they burst into a thousand stars of various hues'. It added that at eleven o'clock the large guns in the square were fired to finish the display (presumably these were the two cannons gifted to Galway a year earlier after they had been captured during the Crimean War by the predecessor regiment of the Connaught Rangers and that are now on display outside the City Hall on College Road). The *Galway Mercury* concluded that 'people retired highly delighted with the evening's entertainment'.

Some Galway people, however, continued to puzzle over the grounding of the *Indian Empire*, and their talk of the incident reached the ears of James Joyce, who put it into the mouths of three characters in Dublin on the morning and evening of its anniversary nearly fifty years later, gaining it a far wider circulation in the twentieth century and the twenty-first.[11] In *Ulysses*, however, Joyce made the claims of the three characters deliberately inaccurate: the first reference is made by the Dalkey schoolmaster, Mr Garret Deasy, an example of an educated man 'who is full of falsehood', as Marilyn French has pointed out;[12] the second and third references occur in the episode set in the cabman's late-night shelter, 'Eumaeus', where almost everything anyone says is questionable and where the *Evening Telegraph* newspaper that Bloom reads contains some obvious errors, 'not forgetting the usual crop of nonsensical howlers and misprints'.

'I am heaping all kinds of lies into the mouth of that sailorman in *Eumeus* which will make you laugh,' Joyce told his friend Frank Budgen when he was writing the chapter.[13] The unreliability of the assertions made in the episode is signalled early on as Bloom and Stephen enter the cabman's shelter. Bloom had whispered a few hints about the keeper's notoriety to Stephen, but, adds the narrator, 'He wouldn't vouch for the actual facts, which quite possibly there was not one vestige of truth in.'

The conspiracy theory has been dismissed far more firmly by the late Mr Justice Adrian Hardiman of the Irish Supreme Court. 'Anti-British prejudice, of which there are many examples in *Ulysses*, leads some characters to conclude that a small marine accident in Galway Bay was caused by British Government 'palmoil' or bribes to the ship's master, in order to suppress the potential of Galway as a transatlantic port,' he wrote, before concluding: 'It is more obviously attributable to negligent navigation.' He added: 'A ship striking an isolated rock *might* be caused by an act of sabotage on the part of her captain, but the mere fact of the accident does not demonstrate this.'[14]

Bloom himself noted in the cabman's shelter that 'when all is said and done, the lies a fellow told about himself couldn't probably hold a proverbial candle to the wholesale whoppers other fellows coined about him'. But he added: 'Mind you, I'm not saying that it's all a pure invention.'

7

AUGHRIM

The Lass of Aughrim and the Lady of Coole

Oh Gregory, let me in
— From *The Lass of Aughrim*

... that old hake Gregory
— *Ulysses* (9:1,066)

I think he has genius of a kind and I like his pride and waywardness ... I am afraid he will knock his ribs against the earth, but he has grit and will succeed in the end.
— Lady Gregory on Joyce in 1902

JOYCE'S SISTERS TOLD ONE BIOGRAPHER, Constantine Curran (a friend from his university days) that 'The Lass of Aughrim' – the key song in 'The Dead' – was one of their brother's favourite ballads. 'Rightly or wrongly,' Curran recalled, 'they laughingly spoke of a sad ballad, "The Lass of Aughrim", which, they said, Joyce was perpetually singing at home. He purported to know 35 verses of it.'[1] One sister, Mrs Eileen Schaurek, who lived for many years with Joyce and Nora and their children in Trieste, recalled: 'For leisure, he would turn to the piano and sing in a clear tenor voice Irish melodies of the sentimental kind.'[2] And Arthur Power, a friend and companion from Joyce's years in Paris, has recalled how at parties in his own apartment Joyce would go to the piano at around midnight when 'he would sing in a light and pleasant tenor voice many Irish ballads in which romance and lament and satire were combined, and which were the secret source of his inspiration'.[3]

Just as the traditional reel 'The Bucks of Oranmore' has little or nothing to do with the village of Oranmore in County Galway (being instead an adaptation of the Scottish reel 'The Bucks of Cranmore'), the ballad 'The Lass of Aughrim' is linked symbolically rather than literally to the east Galway district where the climactic battle of the Williamite Wars in Ireland took place on Sunday, 12 July 1691. The lament – and it did originally comprise thirty-five verses – first emerged in Scotland as either 'The Lass of Roch Royal', 'The Lass of Roch Royall' or 'Isabell of Rochroyall' at the beginning of the eighteenth century.[4]

The treacherous seducer in the song, although unnamed in Joyce's 'The Dead', is a certain Lord Gregory and a well-known alternative version of the song is called 'Lord Gregory'. The two and a half lines of the song that are sung in 'The Dead' are common to both versions, but Joyce stops short of naming the villain.[5] It has been suggested – notably by NUI Galway graduate and academic Frank Shovlin[6] – that Joyce placed the song in 'The Dead' not just to acknowledge Nora Barnacle and her mother, but also to mock Lady Gregory of Coole Park, whose patronage he had sought at the beginning of his career (and who came from the polar opposite stratum of late-nineteenth-century Galway society to Nora Barnacle). In the longer versions of the song the real villain is not Lord Gregory but his mother – a Lady Gregory perhaps.

Lady Augusta Gregory of Coole Park, on the Galway side of Gort, was the wife of Sir William Gregory, an MP for Galway, and earlier for Dublin, and a sometime Governor of Ceylon. Gregory notably proposed what became known as 'The Gregory Clause', an amendment to the 1847 Poor Relief (Ireland) Bill, passed by the House of Commons during the worst year of the Famine, which stipulated that no one who held a lease of more than a quarter of an acre of land should be allowed to enter a workhouse or to avail of any of the Famine relief schemes. 'Mr Gregory's name entered Irish history as a curse,' wrote the historian John Kelly in *The Graves Are Walking*.[7] An earlier Famine historian, Canon John O'Rourke, described it as 'the never-to-be-forgotten quarter-acre-Gregory clause' and said of it that '[a] more complete engine for the slaughter and expatriation of a people was never designed'. In his 1874 book *The History of the Great Irish Famine*, O'Rourke wrote: 'The Gregory Clause should be forever remembered by the descendants of the slaughtered and expatriated small farmers of Ireland.'[8]

A Gregory biographer agreed. 'By his conduct throughout the spring of 1847 Gregory had made his name one of the most detested in Ireland,' wrote Brian Jenkins, noting that 'when the peasants' immediate needs came into conflict with the future interests of his own and already hard-pressed class Gregory's overriding concern was to protect the latter'.[9] He added:

By 1851 a combination of famine deaths and the Gregory clause had greatly eased the landlords' problem of 'redundant population', for many of the tiny smallholdings had disappeared. It was not an achievement Gregory cared to claim, or long savoured, for the image of human misery found on the other side of this legislative coin was to dog his political career for years.[10]

Lady Gregory, however, was not born until after the Famine (in March 1852) and she did not marry Sir William Gregory until 1880, when she was aged twenty-seven years and he was sixty-three (and marrying for the second time, his first wife having died in 1873 after a year of marriage). Sir William, whose grandfather and namesake had been the Under Secretary for Ireland between 1812 and 1831, made his notorious House of Commons intervention when he was a Tory MP for Dublin and before he inherited Coole Park, where he was shocked and distressed by the effects of the Famine. 'There was nothing I ever saw so horrible as the appearance of those suffering from starvation,' he said in his autobiography. 'I well remember the poor wretches being housed against my demesne wall in wigwams of fir branches.'[11]

Nor did his ill repute extend as far as Coole or his neighbouring estate townlands of Kiltartan and Corker. 'The memory of William, or as he is better known "Sir William", lives on with general esteem in Kiltartan,' according to local historian Sister Mary de Lourdes Fahy.[12] 'It was to be his proud claim in 1889 that he had never evicted a tenant in his 42 years as landlord of Coole,' she wrote, citing Galway Diocesan Archives.[13] 'During the Famine', noted another local historian, 'some landlords in the area did not enforce the collection of rents, most notably the De Basterots and the Gregorys.'[14]

Contemporary newspapers agreed. At the end of 1849 the *Tuam Herald* and the *Limerick Examiner* declared:

> Mr Gregory is no longer to be classed among the hard-hearted or oppressive landocracy. He has nobly eschewed their wicked counsels and is resolved to enroll himself in future as a generous landlord and a friend of the poor. Mr Gregory's demeanour convinces one that in his heart there are mercy, charity and benevolence.[15]

Bonfires blazed and people danced in the Square in Gort when Sir William returned from his seven years in Ceylon (now Sri Lanka) in 1878, barely a single generation after the Famine. 'His authorship of the quarter-acre test was slowly forgiven, if not forgotten, at least in Galway,' noted biographer Brian Jenkins.[16] Two and a half years after returning to Coole, Sir William married Augusta, the former Augusta Isabella Persse, seventh daughter of the prominent Persse family from the neighbouring south Galway estate based around Roxborough House, at the foot of the Slieve Aughty mountains near Kilchreest (south of Loughrea on the N66 between Loughrea and Gort).[17] The Roxborough estate comprised 12,000 acres at its peak and Roxborough House was said to have been the first slate-roofed house in County Galway.[18] Augusta's grand-uncle Henry Stratford

Persse established a large brewery and distillery on Nuns' Island, where Gretta Conroy had her last, heart-rending meeting with 'poor Michael Furey', according to her anguished recollection in 'The Dead'.[19] Augusta's uncle, Thomas Moore Persse, ran the distillery in the middle of the nineteenth century, when it was producing up to 400,000 gallons of whiskey a year and supplying the House of Commons in London. He was also a shareholder in the company that owned the Galway Line, which brought the *Indian Empire* into Galway Bay in June 1858.[20] In the same year, her half-brother Dudley Persse of Roxborough and her cousin Burton Persse, of Moyode Castle, Craughwell, were Deputy Lieutenants for County Galway while two other Persses were Galway magistrates. The imposing Woodville House, adjacent to Roxborough, was home to Augusta's brother Henry.

After marrying Sir William Gregory in March 1880, Lady Augusta moved into Coole Park, where she enthusiastically followed her husband's prenuptial advice that 'you can and will do everything in your power to make them [my tenants] love and value us'. She diligently learned the Irish language – an ambition since childhood – and she collected Irish folklore throughout south Galway. She translated, publicised and championed the works of the poet Raftery and the writer and Gaelic League founder Douglas Hyde (later the first President of Ireland). She worked closely with Hyde for the Irish Literary Theatre (forerunner to the Abbey Theatre) and she promoted Raftery in the pages of the weekly Gaelic League journal *An Claidheamh Soluis* and the *Connacht Tribune*. More than sixty years after Raftery's death she searched for and found his previously unmarked grave, and she was the prime mover (and funder) in arranging for a commemorative slab to be placed over the grave in Killeeneen Cemetery – on the road between Kilcolgan and Craughwell – in 1900.[21] She also weaved a translated quatrain from his best-known poem, 'Anois Teacht an tEarraigh', into her play *The Workhouse Ward*, which was first performed in the Abbey Theatre in 1908, and she is likely to have prompted William Butler Yeats to read some translated Raftery poems at a London dinner table where the guests included the American writer Mark Twain.[22]

Raftery, who died ten years before the start of the Famine, was the subject of the first and longest chapter in Lady Gregory's 1903 book *Poets and Dreamers: Studies and Translations from the Irish*, an essay of over 13,500 words in which she included the reminiscences of some of his friends and neighbours and translations from Irish of some of his poems, as well as an account of his funeral. The book also contains several other references to Raftery, as well as a translation of a Douglas Hyde play about him, *An Posadh* (The Marriage) and translations of three other Hyde plays. Hyde's *Love songs of Connaught* (1893) and four books by Lady Gregory were among the hundreds of books Joyce left behind him in Trieste when he moved to Paris in 1920.

Douglas Hyde and William Butler Yeats were prominent guests at the unveiling of the headstone over Raftery's grave in August 1900 and Yeats became a regular and lingering house guest at Coole Park before he bought and renovated a fourteenth-century Norman castle at nearby Thoor, Ballylee. Lady Gregory's Galway townhouse, 47 Dominic St (actually one of the Persse family's Galway townhouses and now the Galway Arts Centre), is close to where Joyce and his family stayed as guests of Nora's uncle, Michael Healy, during their 1912 holiday in Galway.

Joyce, possibly encouraged by Yeats, twice wrote to Lady Gregory seeking cash – firstly in 1902 before travelling to Paris to study medicine (and, in public libraries, literature and philosophy) and secondly in October 1904 before his departure to the Continent with Nora Barnacle. Lady Gregory gave him advice and references, and some cash (none in 1902 and £5.00 in 1904).[23] She also invited him to Coole Park – he did not go – and she arranged for Yeats to entertain and feed him when he travelled through London en route to Paris. 'I think he has genius of a kind and I like his pride and waywardness,' she told Yeats in a letter. She also told Yeats: 'I am afraid he will knock his ribs against the earth, but he has grit and will succeed in the end.'[24]

In return, Joyce a few months later unfavourably reviewed her book *Poets and Dreamers: Studies and Translations from the Irish* in the *Daily Express*, and he is said to have turned up uninvited at a party she

hosted in Dublin and to have snubbed her there. He later acknowledged in a letter to his mother that the *Daily Express* review was 'very
severe',[25] but his brother Stanislaus has said that Joyce 'would never
alter a comma in what he wanted to say either to suit the editor's
views or flatter his patroness'.[26]

Joyce also clashed with Lady Gregory over her insistence on staging Irish plays instead of European works at the Irish Literary Theatre,
which she co-founded (and which led to the establishment of the
Abbey Theatre). Two and a half years before the *Daily Express* review
of *Poets and Dreamers* he wrote and published an essay criticising the
theatre for staging a play by Douglas Hyde, who wrote under the pen
name 'An Craoibhin Aoibhinn' (the delightful little branch). 'The
Irish Literary Theatre must now be considered the property of the
rabblement of the most belated race in Europe,' Joyce wrote of the
decision to stage *Casadh an tSúgáin*, a one-act play by Hyde.[27]

Lady Gregory translated *Casadh an tSúgáin* and three other Hyde
plays in *Poets and Dreamers*. She translated *Casadh an tSúgáin* as *The
Twisting of the Rope* (not 'Twisting of the Rope' as Joyce named it in
the *Daily Express* review) and she said it was 'the first Irish play ever
given in a Dublin theatre'. She added: 'It has been acted many times
since then, in Dublin, in London, in Galway, in Galway Workhouse,
in Cornamona, Ballaghaderreen, Ballymoe and other places. It has
always given great delight.'[28]

In *Poets and Dreamers* she also wrote:

I hold that the beginning of modern Irish drama was in the
winter of 1898, at a school feast at Coole, when Douglas Hyde
and Miss Norma Borthwick acted in Irish in a Punch and Judy
show; and the delighted children went back to tell their parents what grand curses An Craoibhin had put on the baby and
the policeman.[29]

Although Joyce praised the Hyde play in his *Daily Express* review
as 'certainly entertaining', his overall verdict on the book *Poets and*

Dreamers was so unenthusiastic that the newspaper's editor, E.V. Longworth, took the unusual step of appending the initials J.J. to the piece, so as to dissociate himself from it (foreshadowing Gabriel Conroy being identified by his initials on a *Daily Express* book review in 'The Dead').

Stanislaus Joyce has insisted: 'My brother never cared a rap who read him. I think he wrote to make things clear to himself.'[30] Joyce went on to mock Lady Gregory again in *Ulysses* (where Buck Mulligan reminds Stephen about what he wrote 'about that old hake Gregory ... she gets you a job on the paper and then you go and slate her drivel to Jaysus' – see Chapter 4) and in *Finnegans Wake*, as well as in the poem 'Gas From a Burner', his scathing parting shot at the Irish literary and cultural establishment of 1912, in which he called her 'Gregory of the Golden Mouth'. He wrote that poem on his final journey away from Ireland after a Dublin publishing company, Maunsel and Co., reneged on a contract to publish his short story collection *Dubliners*. The same company had published Lady Gregory's *Kiltartan History Book* and *The Kiltartan Wonder Book* as well as works by J.M. Synge and Padraic Colum. Joyce had *The Kiltartan Wonder Book*, along with *Poets and Dreamers* and two other Lady Gregory books, on his bookshelves in Trieste. A limerick that mocks Lady Gregory more humorously has also been attributed to Joyce by Padraic Colum and by Oliver St John Gogarty, although Gogarty himself is as likely to have been the author.

Lady Gregory appears not to have resented Joyce's jibes. 'I did not know I had been thus celebrated,' she wrote in her journal after finding the limerick in a literary magazine that attributed it to Joyce.[31] She also kept a first edition of *Chamber Music* in her Coole Park library and it was from Coole Park that William Butler Yeats successfully lobbied the Royal Literary Fund in 1915 for the grants that became Joyce's first guaranteed regular income as a writer. In 1927 Lady Gregory was among 167 writers and notables, including T.S. Eliot, Ernest Hemingway, Virginia Woolf, Thomas Mann and Albert Einstein, who signed an open letter to several newspapers in Europe and the United States protesting about the publication of a pirated and mutilated version of

Ulysses in the US.[32] In 1931, a little over a year before her death, she wrote in her journal that *A Portrait of the Artist as a Young Man* contained 'here and there a passage of beauty', despite the hardships of the young man's childhood and schooldays. She made no reference to Joyce's mocking her in *Ulysses* and in verse, recalling instead: 'Such a handsome petulant boy he was long ago.'[33]

Frank Shovlin has also suggested that Joyce placed 'The Lass of Aughrim' in his story in a deliberate reminder of the Battle of Aughrim, the last major pitched battle in Irish history and the decisive encounter of the Irish war between King William of Orange and King James, as well as being the impetus for another flight of Wild Geese from Ireland. Lady Gregory wrote in *Poets and Dreamers* that her 'wise old neighbours' still spoke bitterly of the battle and she recalled that the poet Raftery had lamented that 'it was at Aughrim on a Monday that many a son of Ireland found sorrow, without speaking of all that died'. She also included in *The Kiltartan Poetry Book* the lament for the defeat at Aughrim in 'A Blessing on Patrick Sarsfield'. And in *Finnegans Wake* Joyce wrote: 'Forget not the felled! For the lomondations of Oghrem!'[34] Shovlin noted that the phrase *Briseadh Eachdhroma* had become a Gaelic peasants' synonym for disaster and he posited that Joyce 'wished to bring to the surface of his story memories of a defeated Catholic Ireland'. He added that the Battle of Aughrim echo in 'The Dead', the last story in *Dubliners*, bookends a reference to the Battle of the Boyne in the collection's opening story, 'The Sisters'.[35]

Shovlin has also suggested that Joyce's mention of the 'dark mutinous Shannon waves' in the final paragraph of 'The Dead' is a deliberate reference to the last verse of Thomas Davis' well-known ballad 'The West's Asleep':

Sing, Oh! They died their lands to save
At Aughrim's slopes and Shannon's Wave [36]

The suggestion that Joyce's use of 'The Lass of Aughrim' in 'The Dead' was an allusion to Lady Gregory was reinforced in a widely viewed 1987 film adaptation of the story by the famed Hollywood director John Huston, who lived in County Galway, not far from Aughrim, for much of the 1950s and 1960s.[37] Huston, who lived in St Cleran's, an eighteenth-century Georgian manor house near Craughwell, for nearly twenty years, and who partially funded the conversion of the Martello Tower in Sandycove into the James Joyce Museum, inserted into his film a Lady Gregory translation of an old Gaelic poem of betrayal and desertion, 'The Grief of a Girl's Heart' – called 'Donal Óg' in the film – that was not in the text Joyce wrote eighty years earlier in Trieste and Rome. The translation was published in Lady Gregory's 1903 book *Poets and Dreamers: Studies and Translations from the Irish*.

The film's lead female role, the Nora Barnacle character Gretta Conroy, was played by Huston's daughter Anjelica, an Academy Award-winning Hollywood actress who used her memories of her childhood living in St Cleran's and of going to school in Craughwell and Loughrea to help her to portray her character. 'There's a line in "The Dead" which always got me,' she recalled in 1999. 'The line was: "We used to go out walking, Gabriel, the way they do in the country." That's how I remember St Cleran's and growing up in the West. Walks in the night. A whole way of life that's not quite now.'[38]

This line is a slight misquotation of Joyce's text ('We used to go out together, walking, you know, Gabriel, like the way they do in the country'), but she referred to it again ten years later when she told another interviewer:

That line always used to set me off. As soon as I hit that line in that scene I didn't have to work any more. The lines took over ... that's absolutely how it was. I used to go out walking in the rain with Betty O'Kelly, who ran St Cleran's for my father. We'd be walking down the boreens, smoking Player's cigarettes, even when I was a child. It was a very full existence, growing up in the country, getting up to your pursuits.[39]

In her memoir, *A Story Lately Told*, Anjelica said that her first memories were of Ireland and that the sale of St Cleran's in the early 1970s broke her heart and the hearts of her father and brother. She also mentioned many friends 'back home in Ireland'. In her follow-up memoir, *Watch Me*, she said that a recording of the song 'Galway Bay' was used 'to induce my tears' in the TV miniseries *Lonesome Dove*. (However, the first memoir, a *New York Times* bestseller, again misquotes the line from 'The Dead' and the second one places Roscommon 'on the outskirts of Dublin'.)

Anjelica's brother Tony, who also spent much of his youth at St Cleran's, was nominated for an Academy Award for his screenplay of *The Dead*, which was the last film made by their father (who died before it was released). 'It is the most memorable film that I worked on with dad, and it was a story that I had been fascinated with from the time we lived as a family in St Cleran's,' he said.[40]

Draft scripts, as well an extensive collection of other material relating to the film, are among the items in the Huston Archive that was established at NUI Galway in 2010. Welcoming the opening of the archive, Anjelica said: 'It gives me great satisfaction to see that these extensive archives, including remarkable material relating to *The Dead*, have found a permanent place in their rightful home in Galway.'[41] Her sister Allegra said: 'Galway has always held a special place in our hearts.'[42]

8

LUCIA

'A granddaughter of Galway'

Rosefrail and fair – yet frailest
A wonder wild
In gentle eyes thou veilest,
My Blueveined child.
    — From *A Flower Given to My Daughter*

She was a very gentle and sweet creature.
    — James Joyce, 15 December 1940

LUCIA WAS THE YOUNGER OF THE TWO CHILDREN of James Joyce and Nora Barnacle. She was born in Trieste in July 1907, in a pauper's ward (almost like her mother), and named Lucia Anna (Lucia for light and Anna after her Galway grandmother, Annie Barnacle).[1]

In the poem 'A Flower Given to My Daughter', written in Trieste around the same time as 'She Weeps Over Rahoon', Joyce mentions 'my blueveined child', and in *Giacomo Joyce*, which he withheld from publication, he described his daughter as a 'frail, blue-veined child'.

The bond between James Joyce and Lucia was 'one of the most affecting relationships in the whole of modern biography', according to the writer and critic Anthony Burgess. He described Lucia as 'the poor girl who inherited her father's genius in the form of dementia'.[2]

Lucia said that her *Pomes Penyeach* illustrations had been inspired by *The Book of Kells*. She told an interviewer in 1932 that seeing the

Book of Kells had been an event of great importance in her life and that its flowing, rhythmic calligraphy had led her to admire dance, then to learn dance, and finally to let dance guide her pen and brushes.[3]

Her interest in the book was sparked by her father. He said of it:

> In all the places I have been to, Rome, Zurich, Trieste, I have taken it about with me, and have pored over its workmanship for hours. It is the most purely Irish thing we have, and some of the big initial letters which swing right across a page have the essential quality of a chapter of *Ulysses*. Indeed, you can compare much of my work to the intricate illuminations.[4]

Lucia also illustrated her father's *A Chaucer ABC* and some early excerpts from *Finnegans Wake*, as well as family Christmas cards. However, her calligraphy career was short-lived, and it followed her abrupt abandoning of a very promising apprenticeship as a dancer after she had begun to display signs of mental ill health. She was diagnosed with psychosis in 1932 and subsequently spent frequent spells in hospital, interrupted by an unhappy visit to Ireland in 1935. She spent the remainder of her life in institutions and she died in December 1982 in St Andrew's Institution in Northampton.

Joyce had contributed funds towards the publication of some of Lucia's illustrations to try to encourage her. He told Harrier Weaver in 1936:

> My idea is not to persuade her that she is a Cezanne but that on her 29th birthday in the aforesaid madhouse she may see something to persuade her that her whole past has not been a failure. ... The reason I keep on trying by every means to find a solution for her case is that she may not think that she is left with a blank future as well.[5]

He vigorously opposed leaving her in hospital until the worsening world war forced him to flee from German-occupied France with

Nora and his son and grandson in 1940. He had told Harriet Weaver:

> I will not do so as long as I see a single chance of hope for her
> recovery, nor blame her or punish her for the great crime she
> was committed in being a victim to one of the most elusive dis-
> eases known to man and unknown to medicine. And I imagine
> that if you were where she is and felt as she must you would
> perhaps feel some hope if you felt that you were neither aban-
> doned or forgotten.[6]

The German authorities who controlled Vichy France initially
indicated that Lucia would be allowed to travel to Switzerland with
the rest of the family, but they changed their minds as the war wors-
ened and at the last minute only issued four exit visas, for Joyce, Nora,
Georgio and his son Stephen. Joyce made a last, desperate plea to the
Geneva-based Irish acting secretary general of the League of Nations,
Seán Lester, whose name he had been given by the Irish Minister in
France, Seán Murphy. In one of the last letters he wrote before leaving
France, Joyce asked Lester on 10 December if he could get the Red
Cross society in Geneva to intervene on Lucia's behalf. He wrote:

> I shall be very greatly obliged if you can see your way to bring
> my daughter's case under the consideration of the society
> mentioned and thank you in advance for any help you may be
> able to give her and me in this matter.[7]

Joyce met Lester in Geneva a week later en route to Zurich and
he told him that Lucia was 'a very gentle and sweet creature' and that
he had visited her in the sanatorium every weekend. Lester, a former
journalist and Irish diplomat, subsequently sent Joyce an account of
his efforts on Lucia's behalf, but Joyce died on the morning the letter
was being dispatched to him. Lester instead wrote to Nora on that
morning:

Dear Mrs Joyce, I have just received a telephone message from Zurich, telling me of your husband's death. It has been a great shock to me and I want to send at once a message of my deep sympathy. I had just signed the enclosed letter to him.[8]

Giorgio Joyce replied to Lester on Nora's behalf three weeks later, saying that she was 'much too upset to be able to attend to any correspondence' and adding: 'My mother begs me to thank you for all you have tried to do for my sister and wishes to be kindly remembered to you.' He also thanked Lester for 'the beautiful wreath' he had sent to the funeral and he suggested that he might try to get an Irish passport for Lucia. 'Naturally I would like to carry out my father's wishes and have her brought here to Switzerland,' he wrote.[9]

None of the family ever saw Lucia again following her final hospital admission. After the war Nora asked Harriet Weaver to try to get her a copy of Joyce's *A Chaucer ABC* illustrated by Lucia. Evelyn Cotton, a Zurich-based English actress who had been friendly with the Joyces since World War I, later thanked Miss Weaver on Nora's behalf, adding that Mrs Joyce 'was quite upset at seeing it again, as it woke all sorts of memories'.[10]

Lucia visited Galway only twice, as a child in 1912 and as a teenager in 1922 (see Chapter 3). She made a number of attempts to return in adulthood, but was frustrated by her failing health. She planned to visit Galway while holidaying with her cousins in Bray in 1935, but she changed her mind following a chance meeting with one of her Galway aunts, Kathleen Barnacle, in Dublin. Her parents had been worried about her failure to contact them for weeks while she was in Bray and her father had enlisted Michael Healy, in vain, to try to find her. James Joyce told his sister who was hosting Lucia in Bray, Eileen Joyce Schaurek, that Nora 'is not very keen on Lucia's going to Galway as she anticipates trouble when her people find out that she doesn't go to holy mass, holy confession, holy communion and holus bolus'. He added: 'However, she thinks the air will do her good.'[11]

Nearly forty years after her last visit to Ireland, Lucia was still hoping to return, despite having spent most of the intervening years in institutions. In March 1973 she wrote to one of the cousins with whom she had stayed in Bray begging to be brought back there and as late as March 1980 'she spoke of her wish to cross the Irish Sea in a luxurious boat, to stay in a hotel and to visit Galway'.[12]

A few months before her death she sent a note to people in Galway on the occasion of the unveiling of the plaque in memory of her mother on the front wall of the Nora Barnacle House, which was formally opened during the centenary of James Joyce's birth (1982) by the Mayor of Galway (and future President of Ireland) Michael D. Higgins, and the writer and University College Galway English Literature Professor, Tom Kilroy.

This final contact with Galway was through Lucia's guardian, Jane Lidderdale, a godchild and biographer of Joyce's chief patron, Harriet Weaver, who had been Lucia's first guardian after her parents' death. Lucia's note is now in the James Hardiman Library at NUIG with the *Pomes Penyeach* facsimile illustrated with her own initial letters. In a letter accompanying the note, Jane Lidderdale told an NUIG Dean, Mr Mac Lochlainn:

> You have paid Lucia Joyce a very graceful compliment in accepting for custody at University College Galway the note she sent on the occasion of the unveiling on 19th June of the plaque in memory of her mother. I shall be seeing Lucia for her birthday (this month) and will bring your letter with me. She varies very much from visit to visit in the amount of interest she takes in the world outside her ward (where she has a private bedroom). I hope on my next visit she will be ready to hear about the centenary celebrations – and about your copy of *Pomes Penyeach* with her illuminated initials. We have this link – that she is a granddaughter of Galway, and I, or Headford![13]

The note from Lucia was typewritten but signed in her own hand-writing. It said: 'I am very glad my mother is being commemorated in Galway and I send kind regards to everyone.'[14]

Lucia's Galway grandmother, Annie Barnacle, died in November 1940, just as Lucia was being separated irrevocably from her family by illness and the worsening world war. Annie died in November 1940 at No. 4 Bowling Green, in the presence of her daughter Kathleen. The drinks for her wake were purchased from 'J. Young, Mineral Water Manufacturer, Eglinton St and Mary St', the employers four decades earlier of Willie Mulvagh, who would become Molly Bloom's 'Mulvey'. A dispute about Annie's will, which had been lost, was not resolved for a number of years. Her estate was worth over 1,600 pounds (mostly as a result of her having been the sole surviving relative of her bachelor brother, Michael Healy).

Annie Barnacle left the residue after her bequests to her daughter and sole executrix, Kathleen, but the biggest bequest, 100 pounds, went 'to my daughter Mrs Nora Joyce at present residing in Paris, France'. Her solicitor, William Concannon, explained: 'The said Annie Barnacle mentioned that Mrs Joyce and her husband Mr James Joyce had always been good to her.'[15] And Joyce himself said that Mrs Barnacle 'has always been a kind of worshipper of mine and thinks I am a miracle-worker'.[16] He also told Nora after his first visit to Galway that he was very fond of her mother, underlining the word 'very'.[17] Just as Nora and James Joyce were the biggest beneficiaries of Annie's will, James had been the sole legatee (of seven surviving siblings) when his spendthrift father, John Stanislaus Joyce, died in 1931, leaving an estate worth £36.12s.1d.

Mrs Annie Barnacle also left 20 pounds each to her three other children and the same amount to 'Fr Stephenson SJ, Galway, for the celebration of Masses in a church open for public worship in Saorstát Éireann for the repose of the soul of myself and my brother Michael Healy, deceased'. Fr William Stephenson taught in the Jesuit school, St Ignatius College, Sea Road, Galway, from 1920 to 1945. The Jesuit church was not Mrs Barnacle's parish church, but Fr Stephenson would have known Michael Healy well through the men's sodality of Our Lady.

Father Stephenson made annual visits to Galway after he retired. He was born in 1882, the same year as James Joyce, and he died in 1980 on 6 January, the fittingly Joycean Feast of the Epiphany. His Requiem Mass was celebrated in the Jesuit Church on Upper Gardiner Street, Dublin – St Francis Xavier's – the church Joyce described in *Ulysses* as 'the sacred edifice' where Molly Bloom put the other members of the choir 'totally in the shade' with her 'fine voice' singing Rossini's *Stabat Mater*, according to her husband.[18] It is also the church that features in the *Dubliners* stories 'Grace' and 'An Encounter' and into which the young Stephen Dedalus wanders during Good Friday ceremonies in *Stephen Hero*.[19]

Rossini's *Stabat Mater*,[20] which is mentioned a number of times in *Ulysses*, is one of very many musical renditions of the mesmeric medieval Catholic hymn of the same name, 'written by an Italian poet from the Thirteenth Century'.[21] The Latin hymn imagines Mary, the mother of Jesus of Nazareth, standing by his cross at the end of his crucifixion.

Stanza 3 describes Mary as *tristis et afflicta* – sad and afflicted. Sad and afflicted mothers abound in Joyce's life and works. Among them are his own mother, Gogarty's mother and Nora's mother, as well as Gretta Conroy, Molly Bloom, Bertha Rowan, Anna Livia Plurabelle, and Nora, the mother of Giorgio and of Lucia.

9

ZURICH

'Where my dark lover lies'

At the last, amidst a happy folk, shall your own death come to you, softly, far from the salt sea, and make an end of one utterly weary of slipping downward into old age.
— From *The Odyssey,* by Homer[1]

All must go through it, Stephen ... You too. Time will come.
— *Ulysses* (15:4157)

I am passing out. O bitter ending! I'll slip away before they're up. They'll never see. Nor know. Nor miss me.
— From *Finnegans Wake* (page 627)

JOYCE'S 'AFFLICTED MOTHER' APPEARS in *Ulysses* as a ghost who foretells his death and begs him to return to prayer and repentance.[2] She appears in a phantasmagorial passage in the 'Circe' episode and warns her son: 'All must go through it ... You too. Time will come.'

Less than a month before his death, Joyce was asked by the Irish diplomat Seán Lester while en route to Zurich why he had not returned to Ireland. He replied: 'I am attached to it daily and nightly like an umbilical cord.' And Nora and Giorgio affirmed that he listened to Radio Éireann 'all the time'.[3]

But Nora also spoke more prophetically than she knew when she told Lester at the same meeting that the city of Zurich had always been associated with certain crises in their lives and that now they were going back there 'in another crisis'.[4]

The meeting with Seán Lester in the Richemond Hotel in Geneva on Sunday, 15 December 1940, was almost certainly Joyce's last conversation with an Irishman. Four Sundays later was his last full day on earth.

Joyce's unexpected death in exile was reported on the following day in the Galway city weekly *Connacht Sentinel*. The report, on page 2, said:

> James Joyce, the Irish writer whose writings provoked worldwide discussion, died in a Zurich hospital yesterday. Born in Dublin in 1882, he was the son of a Parnellite organizer. He was educated at Clongowes, Belvedere and University College Dublin, later going to Paris where he studied music and medicine.
>
> In 1904 he married Nora, daughter of the late Mr and Mrs Thomas Barnacle, Bowling Green, Galway. A sister, Mrs Mai [*sic*] Monaghan, and a sister-in-law, Mrs Kathleen Griffin, reside in Galway.[5]

An identical report and headline was carried in the following Saturday's *Connacht Tribune*, on page 3, and that weekend's *Galway Observer* also noted the death in a three-paragraph report on page 2.

The Irish State was not represented at the funeral, which was attended by only a small gathering of relatives and friends. 'It was a white and cold day and the sun was pale,' recalled Carola Giedion-Weckler, who accompanied Nora to and from the cemetery.[6] The British consul, Lord Derwent, delivered a eulogy and a Swiss tenor, Max Meili, sang a Handel composition and the lament *Tu Se' Morta* (You are dead) from Monteverdi's seventeenth-century opera *Orpheo*.[7] 'However,' recalled Carola Giedion-Weckler, 'the most striking part of the ceremony came at the end when Nora Joyce had to part from the lowering coffin and with a simple, impulsive gesture spread out her arms for a farewell, while she bent lovingly over the wooden coffin as though to prevent the final lowering.'[8]

Carola Giedion-Weckler also recalled that Nora brought a wreath in the shape of a harp 'entwined with grass-green ribbons'. Another Zurich friend, bank official Paul Ruggiero, who helped procure the Joyce family's entry visas and who had been their friend since their first stay in the city during World War I, also stood beside Nora at the graveside. He recalled: 'There were a number of wreaths but the most beautiful was one from his wife who had ordered a wreath in the form of a harp. She told me, "I had it made in that shape for my Jim because he loved music so much."'[9]

Nora survived without her husband for just over a decade. She continued to live in Zurich, with mostly only her son Giorgio and her sole grandson, Stephen James Joyce, for company. 'My mother has been wonderfully courageous and I hope she will be able to continue being so,' Giorgio wrote to Harriet Weaver two months after Joyce's death.[10] Stephen has recalled that Nora spoke to him in English, whereas she had spoken to her own children in Italian. A neighbour noted that 'not a day went by without a letter or a cutting or a visit of someone wanting her to autograph one of his books'.[11] She replied to one visitor who asked her about another writer: 'Sure, if you've been married to the greatest writer in the world, you don't remember all the little fellows.'[12]

Arthur Power noted that 'her natural spontaneity never deserted her, except after Joyce's death, when, it seemed to me, she deliberately suppressed it'. He recalled her remarking years earlier at a pallid party in Paris: 'If this was happening in Galway, we'd all be out in a minute on the road kicking up our heels in the dust.'[13]

Nora's health worsened in widowhood. Just over a year after James Joyce's death, Harriet Weaver wrote to Nora's sister, Kathleen, in Bowling Green:

Mrs Joyce seems to be in a sad way – not at all well, suffering from bad rheumatism and very lonely, so Georgio said in his letter of December 29th. I hope she will manage to arrange to take the cure of baths which Georgio said she ought to do in the Spring.[14]

Nora herself wrote to Kathleen a short time later: 'I have plenty of worries myself ... Jim's death has been a terrible shock to me ... Lucia is in France ... I have no news of her ... Hope you are well.' The letter, signed 'Nora' and written on notepaper from the Carlton Elite Hotel, Zurich, in April 1942, was sent by airmail and opened by wartime censors.[15]

Eighteen months later Nora told Harriet Weaver: 'We have absolutely no way of communicating with Lucia's doctor in France. As a matter of fact we do not even know where she is. You can imagine how disturbing all this is for us.'[16] She said that all debts arising from her husband's illness and death had been paid 'which left us in a pretty desperate financial condition' and she added: 'It is impossible to get along on the money you were kind enough to advance us, as it is very expensive living here. I have been under the care of doctors for the last two years, as I am suffering from acute rheumatism.'[17]

Nora moved to a *pension* elsewhere in Zurich, where a neighbour observed: 'Of late, arthritis is crippling her. She goes about slowly, at times painfully, with the help of a stick.' In a profile published less than eighteen months before her death, the neighbour, journalist Kees Van Hoek, also noted that 'well-nigh half a century of Continental wanderings (she speaks French, German and Italian fluently) has not blurred her endearing brogue'.[18]

The article went on:

Hers is a lonely life, and once a week she goes up to the Fluntern Cemetery. One morning, I met her there by chance, sitting on a bench underneath the barren silver birches, gazing out on the city spread below along the lake against a backcloth of snowcovered Alpine peaks, and she remarked that the loveliest word in the German language is that for cemetery, *Friedhof*, 'homestead of peace'.[19]

Nora had great difficulty getting any income from the royalties due on her late husband's works in the years during and after World War II. The demand for any material related to him had yet to intensify. A letter from Kathleen in Galway in 1947 informed her that a large cache of her husband's documents left behind in Paris had been presented to the National Library of Ireland. Her friend Evelyn Cotton told Harriet Weaver that Nora was 'extremely upset and put out' that she had not been consulted about the donation. She added: 'Ireland never appreciated James Joyce and she would have preferred the documents to be in England or America.'[20]

Nora's difficult late years are clear in a letter, sent from a less elite address in Zurich, the Hotel Neptun, to her friends Padraic and Mary Colum some time before her final illness. 'Dear Padraic and Molly,' she wrote,

> I really don't know how to thank you and your friends for your very kind gesture in sending me two remittances of 50 and 40 dollars. You can't imagine what a help it is for me to receive some financial aid as I have not received any money from England for seven months except £20. Luckily my solicitor was able to arrange that I get some of the royalties direct from America. It is very difficult for me because I have to support Giorgio who has absolutely not a penny of his own and can't get work here.[21]

So impecunious had Nora become in her final years that she resolved to sell one of her most treasured possessions – a unique copy of *Chamber Music* handwritten by Joyce himself in indelible Indian ink on parchment paper and sent to her as 'a special Xmas present' when he was delayed in Dublin in 1909. Joyce had told Nora that 'this book will last hundreds of years',[22] but she told the Colums: 'I am afraid I shall sooner or later have to sell my manuscript of *Chamber Music* written in Dublin in the year 1909 and dedicated to me; it is written on parchment and bound in cream coloured leather with the Joyce crest on one side of the cover and our initials on the other side.' She went on to ask them: 'If you know anybody who you think will be interested in buying such a work would you kindly let me know.'[23]

Harriet Weaver, meanwhile, worked tirelessly to try to persuade the British authorities to allow royalties to be sent to Nora, who was still a British subject living in Switzerland. She told her own solicitor in London: 'In a letter I had from Miss Cotton dated 20 July she said Mrs Joyce had been so very short of funds that she had parted with a great treasure, a manuscript copy of *Chamber Music* written on parchment for her many years ago by Mr Joyce and specially dedicated to her. Nothing but direct need would have induced her to part with this – which she had entrusted to a friend to take to America and sell to the highest bidder.'[24]

Nora's penury and desperation must have been great. Joyce had told her when he sent her the bound manuscript from Dublin by 'registered, express and insured post':

Perhaps this book I send you now will outlive both you and me. Perhaps the fingers of some young man or girl (our children's children) may turn over its parchment leaves reverently when the two lovers whose initials are interlaced on the cover have long vanished from the earth.[25]

Earlier, while copying the thirty-six poems on the specially cut sheets of parchment, he had written to her: 'I will burn all the other MSS of my verses and you will then have the only one in existence. It is very hard to copy on parchment but I work at it hoping it will give pleasure to the woman I love.'[26]

Nora died in 1951 on 10 April (in the same week that the Irish Censorship of Publications Board revoked the ban on *Stephen Hero* that it had imposed in November 1944). A telegram from Giorgio to Harriet Weaver (MOTHER DEAD THIS MORNING – JOYCE) eerily echoed the one his own father had received in Paris in 1903 (MOTHER DYING COME HOME FATHER).[27]

One of the few people to attend Nora's funeral was family friend Stuart Gilbert, who said she had died 'after a long and painful illness'. He added:

> Nora Joyce had made her confession and had been given the Last Sacraments, and the service at the grave (in German) was according to the Catholic rite. Her son Mr George Joyce, who had settled in Zurich to be with his mother, was the only member of the family present.[28]

Nora's death was reported in the *New York Times* and *The Times* of London and in the then widely read *Time* magazine, but it was overlooked by the weekly *Galway Observer*, published on Abbeygate Street, at the other end of which she had played as a child. The *Connacht Sentinel* placed the news at the top of its front page with a two-deck headline 'Death in Zurich' beneath a bold print underlined strap that said 'Widow of James Joyce'. The *Sentinel* also reverted to spelling her name as it was on her birth certificate and in letters from her mother.

The report said:

> Mrs Norah Joyce, widow of the famous author James Joyce, who died in a Zurich (Switzerland) clinic last week, was a daughter of the late Thomas and Annie Barnacle, Bowling Green, Galway. Mrs Joyce had been suffering from arthritis for a couple of years and her death was hastened when she fell victim to pneumonia.
>
> Mrs Joyce is survived by Georgio (son) and Lucia Joyce (daughter), Thomas Barnacle of Manchester (brother); Mrs Kathleen Griffin, Bowling Green, Galway; Mrs Mary Blackmore, Los Angeles, and Mrs M. Bond, Blackburn, Lancashire (sisters);

Stephen James Joyce (grandson), and by Mrs Georgio Joyce, formerly Miss Ellen-Castor of New York (daughter-in-law).

An additional paragraph, not carried in a shorter report in that weekend's *Connacht Tribune* and containing a number of slight inaccuracies, said:

Mrs Joyce left Galway for Dublin about 40 years ago. She met her writer-husband in the capital and they left Dublin for Switzerland in the spring of 1904. They then moved to Austria and spent a considerable number of years in Trieste. James Joyce died in Zurich in the early spring of 1941. Last Friday his remains were joined by those of his wife in the Flatern [*sic*] Cemetery, Zurich.

Despite occasional calls for the repatriation of their remains, Joyce and Nora are still buried in the Fluntern Cemetery, which is located on a hillside overlooking the city of Zurich, just as Rahoon Cemetery overlooks Galway city.[29] Although buried apart initially for space reasons, they now lie side-by-side in an afterlife similar to the one that Joyce foretold in the words that he gave to Nora as she mourned over the grave of Michael Furey in the poem 'She Weeps Over Rahoon':

Dark too our hearts, O love, shall lie and cold
As his sad heart has lain
Under the moongrey nettles, the black mould
And muttering rain.[30]

Joyce had besought a brighter afterlife for Nora and himself in a letter he sent her more than forty years earlier in which he paid his greatest tribute to her and to Galway – a plea that they might be reincarnated together in her native county. He regularly called her 'my beautiful wild flower of the hedges' or 'my dark-blue, rain-drenched flower' or 'a wild flower blowing in a hedge' – words he also used to describe Molly in *Ulysses* and Bertha in *Exiles* – and in a letter to Nora four years before he wrote the Rahoon poem, he told her he hoped that they might be reunited forever in Galway after they both had 'long vanished from the earth'.[31]

'I would pray', he told her, 'that my soul be scattered in the wind if God would but let me blow softly for ever about one strange lonely dark-blue rain drenched flower in a wild hedge at Aughrim or Oranmore.'[32]

NOTES

1 – *Wife*

1   In his final weeks in Ireland, Joyce was in Galway from 17 July to 17 August and in Dublin from 17 August to 11 September (Ellmann, *Selected Letters*).

2   Two biographies of Nora were published in the 1980s: *Nora Barnacle Joyce: A Portrait*, by Padraic OLaoi; and *Nora: The Real Life of Molly Bloom*. A movie based on the early chapters of this book, covering the first eight of the thirty-seven years that Joyce and Nora spent together, was released in 1999 by Volta Films. It starred Ewan McGregor and Susan Lynch.

3   5 September 1909, Ellmann, *Selected Letters*, p. 169.

4   25 October 1909, Ellmann, *Selected Letters*, p. 173.

5   *Giacomo Joyce* was written and set in Trieste in 1914, but not published until 1968.

6   LINCHPIN: The word of Richard Ellmann, the pre-eminent Joyce biographer and scholar.

7   The Nora Barnacle house at No. 4 Bowling Green has been preserved by two Galway sisters, Mary and Sheila Gallagher, who bought it in 1987 and who now open it to the public occasionally, having maintained it as a museum for more than twenty years without any civic or State support. A plaque was unveiled on the front of the house in 1982 – the centenary of Joyce's birth – by University College Galway's Modern English Professor Thomas Kilroy and Michael D. Higgins, the then Mayor of Galway and future President of Ireland. The Gallagher sisters marked Bloomsday each year from 1988 onwards with public readings in the house. In recent years the house has rarely been opened. A note on the front window, signed by Mary Gallagher in advance of Bloomsday 2015, said that 'due to repairs necessary to the house, it cannot be opened at this time'.

8   The pro-cathedral, a cut limestone building at the corner of Middle Street and Lower Abbeygate Street, was deconsecrated in 1965 and is currently used as shops and offices.

9   The name Nuns' Island can be traced to the beginning of the nineteenth century. This inland island is bounded by rivulets and narrow tributaries of the River Corrib and the Eglinton Canal. It is directly across the river from Bowling Green in the middle of Galway city. The first nunnery was established there in the mid-seventeenth century on lands known as Illanaltenagh, or Oileán Altanach, meaning 'the island of the flocking birds'.

10 *Irish Times*, 15 November 2003.

11 JJ to SJ, 7 February 1905.

12 Power, *Conversations with James Joyce*, p. 90.

13 Richard Ellmann interview with Eva Joyce, 1953, cited in Ellmann, *James Joyce*, p. 156.

14 'My mother was slowly killed, I think,' Joyce told Nora, 'by my father's ill-treatment, by years of trouble, and by my cynical frankness of conduct' (JJ to NB, 29 August 1904).

15 Curran, *James Joyce Remembered*, p. 70. Anthony Burgess agreed. 'James's need for Nora was beyond all fancy,' he wrote. 'She was unliterary, had no patience with her husband's bizarre projects (why couldn't he write an ordinary story that people could understand?), but she is firmly planted in both *Ulysses* and *Finnegans Wake* – not biographically but mythically. Joyce saw in her the essential virtues of woman. She was down-to-earth, anti-romantic, common-sensical, loyal, forgiving. If Stanislaus was his foil, she was his complement' (Burgess, *Here Comes Everybody*, p. 30).

16 Gilbert, Introduction to *Letters of JJ*.

17 Gorman, *James Joyce*.

18 O'Connor, *The Joyce We Knew*.

19 Ryan, *A Bash in the Tunnel*, p. 186.

20 Colum, *Our Friend James Joyce*, pp. 114–15.

21 Ryan, *New Republic*, 13 May 1931.

22 Kenneth Reddin, *Irish Times*, 14 January 1941.

23 Potts, *Portraits of the Artist in Exile*.

24 From *James Joyce: A Memoir*, Hudson Review 1949–50, quoted in Maddox, *Nora*.

25 In *Finnegans Wake* Anna Livia says: 'Where you meet I. The day. Remember! Why there that moment and us two only? I was but teen, a tiler's dot' (p. 626).

26 Bloom here notices that Stephen is mumbling some lines of poetry, but he fails to recognise the lines, which are from an early W.B. Yeats poem 'Who goes with Fergus?'. This poem had special significance for Joyce, as he sang a version of it that he had put to music for his mother and for his youngest brother when they were on their deathbeds, accompanying himself on piano. In *Ulysses* the ghost of Stephen's mother reminds him, 'You sang that song to me. *Love's bitter mystery*.' Early in *Ulysses*, Buck Mulligan recites that line and two others from the poem after he and Stephen had argued in the Martello Tower about Stephen's failure to kneel and pray at his mother's deathbed. And Stephen himself later recites a line from it – 'And no more turn aside and brood' – while he lies on a rock on Sandymount Strand in the 'Proteus' episode. Joyce's mother was predeceased by her youngest son, Georgie, who, as he lay dying of peritonitis, aged fourteen years, after contracting typhoid, asked James to sing for him his version of the Yeats poem. 'Jim went downstairs to the parlour, and, leaving the doors open, sat down at the piano and sang the melancholy chant to which he had set the verses,' recalled Stanislaus (*My Brother's Keeper*, p. 143). James Joyce subsequently named his only son Giorgio, after his dead youngest brother. He also handwrote another early Yeats poem, 'Down by the Sally Gardens', in one of the letters he wrote to Nora in the months after they met.

27 The words 'Finn's Hotel' are still visible in large white lettering on the gable end of the building, which is on Leinster Street South at the east end of Nassau Street (in 1904 the address was Nos 1 and 2 Leinster Street). Joyce's friends were told that Nora was working in 'one of the better hotels in Dublin' (Colum, *Our Friend James Joyce*, p. 72). The absence of an apostrophe from the title *Finnegans Wake* makes it a pun of many layers, one of which is a reference to Finn's Hotel. Other suggestions include: Finn, again!, Mister Finnagain! And Timm Finn again's (all used in the text); Finnegans awaken; 'Finnegan's Wake' (the nineteenth-century ballad about the wake of the Dublin hod-carrier Tim Finnegan); Fionn Uisce (the Gaelic name for the Phoenix Park, which adjoins Chapleizod, through which the River Liffey flows); Fionn Mac Cumhail (Finn MacCool! in the text) and Finn's Hot. Finn's Hotel is also mentioned in *Ulysses*, in the 'Wandering Rocks' episode.

　　The happenstance of their meeting, and Joyce's persistence in seeking a date with Nora after she had failed to turn up for the first appointment he made, has an echo that was noted by Fritz Senn in Galway in the *Dubliners* short story 'A Painful Case' where Joyce wrote of Mr James Duffy: 'Meeting her a third time by accident he found courage to make an appointment.' Joyce told Nora in a letter (31 August 1909) that when he first courted her 'you were only nineteen', but this seems a mistake since she would have been two months past her twentieth birthday in June 1904.

28 '60 Shellburn' is how he puts it in *Finnegans Wake*.

　　He stayed on the night of 16 June at No. 22 Dromard Avenue, closer to the Star of the Sea Church and Sandymount Strand, where the 'Nausicaa' episode of *Ulysses* is set.

29 JJ to NB, 21 August 1909.

30 '[E]loping for that holm in Finn's Hotel Fiord' is mentioned in *Finnegans Wake*, but much of the text is largely incomprehensible to most readers. Joyce filled more than fifty notebooks with words and phrases when he was composing *Finnegans Wake* in Paris between 1922 and 1939. The notebooks are stored in the State University of New York at Buffalo (the same place as the notes for *Exiles*, see Chapter 2) and facsimiles are held in various libraries, including the National Library of Ireland. Researchers in the US and Europe have spent decades attempting to link the notes to the source material Joyce used, principally the *Encyclopaedia Brittanica*, the *Catholic Encyclopaedia* and various newspapers, including the *Connacht Tribune*, and the *Irish Times* and *Irish Independent*. Transcriptions of two of the notebooks, searchable online under Genetic Joyce Studies, link references in the notebooks to a succession of issues of the *Connacht Tribune* from February, March, April, May, June and July 1924. One of these notebooks has ten items linked to the *Connacht Tribune* and the other one has nine. Joyce copied words and phrases from news reports, court cases, letters to the editor and advertisements in at least eleven separate issues of the newspaper. Most of the notes are in his own handwriting, which

had deteriorated badly as his eyesight failed, and a few are in Nora's handwriting. The copies of the *Connacht Tribune* were probably sent to him by Annie Barnacle. The first notebook, called *Scribbledehobble* after the first word in it, mentions 'Nora Diamond (rough)' on a page headed 'Exiles'. The page headed 'Cyclops' contains 'Raftery, sight was loss on him: J. Joyce, Cuchulan, Mayor of Galway'. And, on a page headed 'Names', it lists 'Mainguard St Galway: Connacht Tube & Tram News'. Few, if any, of the references to Galway in *Finnegans Wake* – Joyce's most difficult work, by some distance – can be linked directly to the *Connacht Tribune*. Very few appear in any meaningful context. Bowling Green is 'bawling green' (p. 517) and Galway is 'gullaway' (p. 197) or 'Dalway' (p. 140). 'The barony of Bohermore', as well as Gort, Coole, Barna, Aran, Salt Hill, Nile Lodge and Portiuncula are mentioned, but without having any obvious meaning. The same applies to 'the warden of Galway', 'the Galwegian caftan', 'the blackfaced connemaras', 'the claddagh ringleaders', 'the Claddagh clasp!' and 'her fancy claddaghs'. A reference to the Maamtrasna murders of 1882 is introduced as 'the wasnottobe crime conundrum'. Myles Joyce is recognisable only as 'a child of Maam' and he is tried under the name 'Festy King' at the Old Bailey in London instead of at Green Street Courthouse in Dublin, where the trial took place. The Galway accent is mimicked perfectly in the phonetic spelling of the word equal as 'aequal' and later 'Aequalllllll!' The Spanish Arch seems to be represented by 'Spanish Place' and the word sequence 'Mayo I make, Tuam I take, Sligo's sleek but Galway's grace' may mean that while Sligo is sleek, Galway is grace. Towards the end of his life, Joyce himself was able to joke about the obtuseness of *Finnegans Wake*. Asked by the former journalist and diplomat Seán Lester if it was a big book, he replied: 'That reminds me of the story of the drunken Irishman walking from Drogheda to Dundalk and when questioned as to the length of the road said it was not the length that worried him, it was the width!' (Seán Lester, 1941 Diary, DCU).

31   JJ to SJ, 12 July 1905.

32   Exactly three months after Joyce met Nora, and one month before they eloped together from Dublin's North Wall, the *Irish Homestead* magazine published his short story 'Eveline', in which a young woman agonises at the North Wall Quay over whether or not to sail into exile with her lover 'to a distant unknown country'. The young woman, he wrote, 'prayed to God to direct her, to show her what was her duty'. Joyce had already lived in Paris for several months, but his and Nora's bravery and singlemindedness in venturing to Eastern Europe in 1904 is underlined in the official statistics for emigration from Ireland, which show that of the 39,902 people who sailed away in that year only twelve others apart from Joyce and Nora went to destinations other than North America, Britain or the rest of the British Empire. See *Irish Historical Statistics: Population 1821–1971*, published by the Royal Irish Academy in 1978, cited in Laffan, 'Bloomsyear: Ireland in 1904' in Fogarty and O'Rourke (Eds), *Voices on Joyce*.

33 Programme Notes for the English Players in Barry, *James Joyce: Occasional, Critical and Political Writing*, p. 209.

34 Postcard: A copy is on display in the Joyce Museum in Trieste, near where the Grand Canal is flanked by a 'Passaggio Joyce' and by a life-size statue of Joyce.

35 JJ to NB, 21 August 1912. Ballybrit: The blue was to represent the sea and the white letters signified the islands Ulysses visited. The other two main characters in Joyce's novel would also be modelled on noble Grecians, Penelope and Telemachus, the wife and son, respectively, of Odysseus. One of Joyce's epiphanies deals with a race meeting, but it was written a decade before his Ballybrit visit. Twenty-two years after his Ballybrit visit, Joyce told a Dublin friend: 'The only decent people I ever saw at a racecourse were the horses' (Letter, 20 December 1934). A day that W.B. Yeats spent at Ballybrit in 1908 resulted in the sixteen-line poem 'At Galway Races', written at Coole Park.

36 'Who ever anywhere will read these written words?' wonders a downcast Stephen in the 'Proteus' episode of *Ulysses* (Slote, *Ulysses: Annotated*, p. 38).

37 JJ to Grant Richards, 23 June 1906.

38 JJ to NB, 21 August 1912. These words strongly echo a phrase Joyce used in his breakthrough publication, his review of Henrik Ibsen's play *When We Dead Awaken*, published in the prestigious London-based *Fortnightly Review* when he was aged only eighteen years and still at university. Referring to Ibsen in the lengthy review, Joyce wrote: 'Many years more, however, must pass before he will enter his kingdom in jubilation' (Gorman, *James Joyce*, p. 66).

39 'Joyce returned to Trieste and never allowed himself to go to Ireland again,' was Richard Ellmann's summary (*Selected Letters*, p. 38). As early as 1906, Joyce had written to Stanislaus: 'I am content to recognize myself an exile: and, prophetically, a repudiated one' (JJ to SJ, 6 November 1906).

   A parallel for the renewed exile – culminating in landlocked Paris, at the urging of Ezra Pound, a travelling American, and the publication there of *Ulysses* by another expatriate American, Sylvia Beach – is to be found foretold twice in Homer's *Odyssey*, Book XI and Book XXIII, where the blind seer Tiresias tells Odysseus he will have to go overland on foot and then adds: 'You must go out one more time.|Carry your well-planed oar until you come|To a race of people who know nothing of the sea,|Whose food is never seasoned with salt, strangers|To ships with their crimson prows and long slim oars,|The wings that make ships fly. And here is your sign –|Unmistakable, clear, so clear you cannot miss it:|When another traveller falls in with you and calls|That weight across your shoulder a fan to winnow grain,|Then plant your bladed, balanced oar in the earth|And sacrifice fine beasts to the lord god of the sea,|Poseidon ...' (Book XI, 138–49 in Fagles and 135–44 in Fitzgerald, *The Odyssey*. Also Book XXIII, 298–310).

   The translation of the Book XI passage by T.E. Lawrence (Lawrence of Arabia) reads: 'Go forth under your shapely oar till you come to a people who know not the sea and eat their victuals unsavoured with its salt; a people ignorant of pur-ple-prowed ships and of the smoothed and shaven oars which are the wings of a ship's flying. I give you this token of them, a sign so plain that you cannot miss it: you have arrived when another wayfarer shall cross you and say that on your doughty shoulder you bear the scatterer of haulms, a winnowing-fan.'

'Ireland is more than Dublin,' observed the writer and critic Anthony Burgess in reviewing 'The Dead'. 'Life may seem to lie in exile, "out in Europe", but it is really waiting coiled up in Ireland, ready to lunge from a wilder west ...' (Burgess, *Here Comes Everybody*, p. 43).

A portrait of Nora was prominently displayed in each of the apartments the couple successively lived in. It was painted in 1913 by the Triestine artist Tullio Silvestri, who told Richard Ellmann that Nora was the most beautiful woman he had ever seen.

40 JJ to SJ, 21 August 1909.

41 *Finnegans Wake*, p. 407.

42 JOYCE TRIBE: In his *History of Galway*, James Hardiman says of the Joyce tribe: 'This old Galway family is of ancient and honourable English descent ... a race of men remarkable for their extraordinary stature, who, for centuries past inhabited the mountainous district, in Iar Connacht, called, from them, Duthaidh Sheod-hoigh, or Joyce Country, now forming the barony of Ross, in the County of Galway.' Hardiman also records – in a coincidence that James Joyce would have relished – that the estate of Rahoon was once owned by a Galwegian goldsmith named Joyce (who had learned the trade during the fourteen years he spent as a captive slave in Algiers before being freed following the intercession of King William III, whose army triumphed at the Battle of Aughrim).

43 JJ to James B. Pinker, 29 July 1918.

44 Joyce regarded 8 October – the day he sailed from Dublin with Nora in 1904 – as his wedding anniversary, according to the director of the first school in Pola where he taught, Allesandra Francini Bruni (in Potts, *Portraits of the Artist in Exile*).

45 JJ to SJ, 2 May 1905. In *Exiles* Richard refers to his and Bertha's son as 'our godless nameless child' and 'a child of sin and shame!' In *Ulysses* 'a medley of voices' called The Sins of the Past say of Bloom that 'he went through a form of clandestine marriage'.

46 JJ to NB, 31 August 1909.

47 Two letters in which Joyce looks forward to and back on his unsuccessful attempts to avoid publicity for the wedding can be viewed online on the National Library of Ireland website. Articles about the wedding appeared on RTE.ie and *Connacht Tribune* on 1 August 2014 and on the National Library blog (October 2014).

48 During their London nuptial sojourn the Joyces lived in Campden Grove, Kens-ington, just off Kensington Church Street and around the corner from Campden Hill Square, which became Britain's most expensive residential street in 2011, with each of its fifty-nine terraced houses worth between £5 million and £10 million, according to Lloyds TSB Bank. 'This part of London has always had a glamorous

reputation, attracting buyers from the business and entertainment world, and more recently the super-rich from across the world,' explained Lloyds TSB economist Suren Thiru (*The Guardian*, 29 December 2011).

49 JJ to GJ, 9 July 1931.

50 Ibid.

51 Lynd, *Galway of the Races*.

52 O Laoi, *Nora Barnacle Joyce*, p. 107.

53 JJ to HSW, 22 March 1940.

54 JJ to Con Curran, 4 October 1936.

55 JJ to Aunt Josephine, 10 November 1922.

56 John Stanislaus Joyce to JJ, 31 January 1931.

57 Ellmann, *Selected Letters*, p. 45.

58 Ellmann, *James Joyce*, p. 737.

59 Gilbert, Introduction to *Letters of James Joyce*.

60 Ellmann, *Selected Letters*, p. 263.

61 JJ to HSW, 1 May 1935.

62 JJ to Mayor of Zurich, 20 December 1940. A postcard to his brother Stephen four days before being taken to hospital was his last written communication.

63 Seán Lester Diary, DCU.

64 Potts, *Portraits of the Artist in Exile*.

2 – Gretta

1 Ellmann, *Selected Letters* (JJ to NB, 22 August 1909), p. 163.

2 JJ to NB, 26 September 1904.

'Gretta Conroy has the Galway firmness of character of her prototype, Nora Joyce,' wrote Anthony Burgess, 'she is beautiful' (Burgess, *Here Comes Everybody*, p. 43).

3 JJ to NB, 31 August 1909.

4 JJ to NB, 26 August 1909.

5 The Bodkin family vault is the first vault on the left on the walkway leading from the old gate of Rahoon Cemetery. The inscription on the vault says: 'Erected by Patrick and Winifred Bodkin in loving memory of their dearly beloved son Michael Marin Bodkin who died 11th of February 1900 aged 20 years. Lord Jesus deliver him comfortress of the afflicted and intercede for him. The Lord gave and the Lord hath taken away. Blessed be the name of the Lord. Job 1:21' (Ó Domhnaill, *Gone the Way of Truth: Historic Graves of Galway*, p. 75). The fictional Michael Furey may also be based on a composite of Michael 'Sonny' Bodkin and an earlier Galway boyfriend of Nora, Michael Feeney, who lived at William Street West and who died in 1897, aged sixteen years, when Nora was not yet aged thirteen. Both men are buried in Rahoon Cemetery.

6   JJ to SJ, 3 December 1904.

7   Quoted in Maddox, *Nora*, from Eilis Dillon, 'The Innocent Muse', unpublished transcript of an interview that appeared, shortened, in *JJQ*, 20:1 (Fall, 1982).

8   JJ to SJ, 7 August 1912.

9   JJ to John Howley, 29 July 1935.

10   It was put on public display in the library on Culture Night in September 2012.

11   JJ to LJ, September 1935.

12   Joyce's handwritten punctuation on the NUIG copy is absent from the sculpted version of the poem erected at the entrance to Rahoon Cemetery by Galway City Council in 2012.

13   See McCourt, *The Years of Bloom*, p. 240. 'On Thursday', the *Connacht Tribune* reported (Saturday, 20 July 1912), 'the Galway Regatta was held under the happiest auspices, and although the morning was rather wild, the afternoon was beautifully fine, and the famous Corrib was crowded with craft of all descriptions. The Grand Stand at Menlo Castle was filled with a large and fashionable gathering.'

14   JJ to AB, 15 October 1936.

15   EMILY: Herring, *Notesheets*, 498, cited in *James Joyce Online Notes*, March 2013. Joyce's notes for *Exiles* were not published until 1951, the year Nora died.

16   If October 1904 is taken as the year of Joyce and Nora's marriage, then 'summer of the year 1912' would have been the middle of their 'seven-year itch' (though the phrase did not become widespread until decades later).

     A three-act Lady Gregory play about a love triangle, *Grania*, was published in 1912, a year before Joyce started to write *Exiles*. It was never staged by the Abbey Theatre.

     W. B. Yeats told Joyce that he would not recommend *Exiles* to the Abbey Theatre. It was staged in the Abbey's sister space, the Peacock Theatre, in 1973 for twenty performances. It was staged at the National Theatre in London in 2006. It has never been staged by the Druid Theatre Company, which is based little more than a stone's throw from Nora Barnacle's childhood homes in Bowling Green and Whitehall.

17   Anthony Burgess' appraisal was: 'Bertha really comes out of it very well: we gain a fleeting glimpse of Nora Joyce as one of the great heroines of our time' (Burgess, *Here Comes Everybody*, p. 77).

18   Missing Nora while in Dublin in 1909, he wrote to her that her eyes 'seem to me like strange beautiful, blue wild-flowers growing in some tangled rain-drenched hedge' (JJ to NB, 19 November 1909). He used the rain-drenched hedge analogy several times in letters to Nora in November and December 1909.

19   BERTHA'S OBSERVATION: *Exiles* in Levin (Ed.), *A James Joyce Reader*, p. 611.

     MEN OF GENIUS: Joyce made this remark in a lecture on the English poet William Blake that he delivered at the Universita Popolare, Trieste in March 1912.

     Nino Frank (in Potts, *Portraits of the Artist in Exile*) claimed that *Pomes* was 'the only part of Joyce's works that Nora knew and appreciated'.

20 Anna was Lucia Joyce's second name. Plurabelle can be loosely translated as 'many-times beautiful' or 'beautiful in many ways'.
21 *FW*, p. 202.
22 *FW*, p. 95.
23 The text says 'Kitty Coleraine of Butterman's Lane' (*FW*, p. 210) and Kitty Cole-raine did spill buttermilk in the song.

George Bernard Shaw said in 1950 that he never had time to 'decipher' *Finne-gans Wake* and Stanislaus Joyce described early excerpts as 'drivelling rigmarole' (Ellmann, *James Joyce*, p. 443, p. 261). Oliver St John Gogarty said it was 'catalectic' (a syllable short!) and Ezra Pound also said he could not understand it (letter, 24 November 1926). The *Irish Press* declared it 'unfinished' two years after it had been published (*Irish Press*, January 1941).
24 Also the list of Catholic priests and their parishes in the Diocese of Galway and *Thom's Directory* 1900/01.
25 JJ to SJ, 3 December 1904.
26 JJ to NB, 19 August 1912, two days after he left Nora in Galway while he returned to Dublin.
27 *FW*, p. 430.
28 *FW*, p. 115.
29 *FW* Notebook, VI.B.5.
30 See Gorman, *James Joyce*, and also Bruce Bradley SJ, 'Something about Tullabeg' in *Studies*, Summer 2004 and 'At School Together in Conmee's Time: Some Notes on Joyce's Clongowes Jesuits' in *Dublin James Joyce Journal*, No. 3, 2010.
31 'I offended two men today by leaving them coolly. I wanted to hear your voice, not theirs,' he wrote to Nora on 15 August 1904. Two weeks later he told her: 'Certain people who know that we are much together often insult me about you. I listen to them calmly, disdaining to answer them but their least word tumbles my heart about like a bird in a storm' (JJ to NB, 29 August 1904).

3 – Lips

1 The full sentence reads: 'I leave for Cork tomorrow morning but I would prefer to be going westward, towards those strange places whose names thrill me on your lips, Oughterard, Claregalway, Coleraine, Oranmore, towards those wild fields of Connacht in which God made grow "my beautiful wild flower of the hedges, my dark-blue rain-drenched flower"' (11 December 1909). Three months earlier he had written to her from her mother's house in Bowling Green: 'Who knows, darling, but next year you and I may come here. You will take me from place to place and the image of your girlhood will purify again my life' (26 August 1909).
2 JJ to NB, 24 December 1909.
3 Ibid.

4   Barry, *James Joyce: Occasional, Critical and Political Writings*, p. 340.

5   The building, at the junction of Shop Street and Upper Abbeygate Street, is the last intact medieval townhouse in Ireland and a national monument. It was purchased in 1918 by the Munster and Leinster Bank and it came into the possession of Allied Irish Banks in 1966.

6   Hardiman, *The History of Galway*, pp. 73–80.

7   The engraving, which Hardiman said was 'taken by an ingenious artist, brought from Dublin solely for the purpose', was not included in his *History of Galway* but it is included in a bound volume of engravings, James Hardiman, 'Sketches of Galway', 1812–30, in the Galway County Council Archives (www.galway.ie/archives).

8   See O'Neill, *The Tribes and Other Galway Families*.

9   Three years after Joyce wrote about Galway city's dilapidation George Bernard Shaw was told, while having his hair cut in the city, that a German warship had sailed into Galway Bay, 'but when the admiral put up his spy glass and saw the ruins, he said: "We must have been here already" and sailed away' (Lady Gregory, *Seventy Years*, p. 522).

10   There are no Spanish Armada wrecks at the bottom of Galway Bay. One vessel, according to tradition, anchored off Barna for a number of days before returning to sea without most of its crew. The name of the vessel, or of its captain, have not been recorded. Two other ships are believed to have floundered off the north Connemara coast. Survivors were brought to Galway city and executed on the orders of the Governor of Connaught, Sir Richard Bingham. They are buried in Forthill Cemetery, where the Spanish Ambassador to Ireland unveiled a plaque in their memory in 1988, four centuries after their burials (Douglas, *The Downfall of the Spanish Armada in Ireland*; and Hart-Davis, *Armada*).

     Joyce's sometime friend and adversary, Oliver St John Gogarty, did not share Joyce's benign view of the fate of the Spanish Armada sailors in Galway. 'The way the survivors were treated on the west coast of Ireland is one of the disgraces of history,' he wrote, adding that the Irish natives 'despoiled them, stripped and clubbed them to death, having robbed them of their silks and jewels' (Gogarty, *Rolling Down the Lea*).

11   The British historian and broadcaster Robert Kee strongly echoed Joyce's conclusion eighteen years later, declaring: 'Though the executed man had nothing to do with political nationalism, he may perhaps stand in the allegory as a martyr for what happened to Ireland over the centuries under English rule' (Waldron, *Maamtrasna: The murders and the mystery*).

12   JJ to NB, 26 August 1909.

13   JJ to Aunt Josephine, 23 October 1922.

14   Ibid.

15   JJ to T.S. Eliot, 1 January 1932.

16   JJ to HSW, 7 April 1935.

4 – Mulvey

1   'A Portrait of the Artist', not to be confused with *A Portrait of the Artist as a Young Man*, was an essay Joyce wrote in January 1904 for the magazine *Dana*, whose editors rejected it. Some of it was refashioned in *Stephen Hero* and later in *A Portrait of the Artist as a Young Man*.

2   MASTERWORK: Few would dispute the use of this superlative. The *Sunday Times* (30 November 2014) described *Ulysses* as 'the 20th century's most dangerous, brilliant book'. *Time* magazine (29 January 1934) dubbed it 'one of the most monumental works of the human intelligence' and 'a work of genius'. The Literary Editor of the *Observer*, Robert McCrum, wrote: 'Novelists working 100 years later still write in the shadow of this extraordinary achievement' (3 August 14). A poll of authors and writers by the US magazine *Book* to ascertain 'the best fictional characters of the 20th Century' put three characters from *Ulysses* in the Top 10: Leopold Bloom at No. 4, Molly Bloom at No. 8 and Stephen Dedalus at No. 9 (*The Guardian*, 6 April 2002). The *Times Literary Supplement*, London, decreed: 'James Joyce was and remains almost unique among novelists in that he published nothing but masterpieces' (quoted on the cover of Joyce's *Stephen Hero*).

3   See Birmingham, *The Most Dangerous Book*, p. 15.

4   Richard Ellmann in Introduction to *Selected Letters*, Vol. 3.

5   MOORISH WALL/SPANISH ARCH: See Maddox, *Nora*, p. 206. A more tenuous Galway reference in Molly's monologue are her two mentions of Algeciras, a Spanish seaport near Gibraltar, 'the true birthplace of Marian Tweedy', who grew up to become Molly Bloom. The Algeciras Stall at the Araby Bazaar held at the RDS in Dublin in 1894 to raise funds for Dublin hospitals was also called 'The Galway Stall' because it was staffed by women from Galway. The *Dubliners* story 'Araby' is about a pre-teenage boy who goes to the Araby Bazaar to buy a gift for a girl he desperately wants to impress – James Joyce was aged twelve in 1894 and he visited the bazaar after travelling by train from his home in the north inner city, as the boy in the story does (Costello, *John Stanislaus Joyce*, p. 129). Joyce described 'Araby' as one of the 'stories of my childhood' (JJ to SJ, 25 September 1905).

6   JJ to SJ, 9 October 1906.

7   STAR TURN: 'Penelope is the clou of the book' (letter, 16 August 1921). Richard Ellmann translated 'clou' as 'star turn' or topper.

8   JOKING J: A couplet from the ballad is recited in the 'Circe' episode by 'Edward the Seventh': 'My methods are new and are causing surprise|to make the blind see I throw dust in their eyes.'

9   STOPPED CLOCK: 'The solemnization of dates came naturally to Joyce,' noted Anthony Burgess (Burgess, *Here Comes Everybody*, p. 17). The 'marble timepiece' also appears in the 'Circe' episode, where its doors open to the sound of 'Cuckoo Cuckoo Cuckoo' in reference to Bloom being a cuckold.

10 Fritz Senn, founder and proprietor of the Zurich James Joyce Foundation, in a paper delivered at Galway City International Heritage Conference, Town Hall Theatre, Galway, on 25 September 2014.

11 PAST: Mulvey is first identified in a letter Joyce sent his brother Stanislaus less than two months after he eloped with Nora. 'She used to go out with Mulvey (he was a Protestant) and walk about the roads with him at time[s]. Says she didn't love him and simply went to pass the time. She was opposed at home and this made her persist' (JJ to SJ, 4 December 1904).

'I am absurdly jealous of the past', Joyce told Nora on the eve of his first visit to Galway in August 1909, 'to see your people.' In a letter he said: 'I wrote today to your mother but really I don't want to go. They will speak of you and of things unknown to me. I dread to be shown even a picture of you as a girl for I shall think "I did not know her then nor she me. When she sauntered to mass in the morning she gave her long glances sometimes to some boy along the road. To others but not to me"' (JJ to NB, 21 August 1909).

12 The Abbey is a Franciscan church and Nora's friend spent her evenings there at around the same time that the teenage James Joyce's alter ego, Stephen Dedalus, was seeking solace in the Dublin churches of the Franciscans and their confrères the Capuchins.

13 Had Joyce looked at a *Connacht Tribune* during either of his two visits to Galway, he could not have missed a prominent, illustrated advertisement for Young's Soda Water. Usually on the top half of the front page, the advertisement showed a large bottle with a diamond-shaped label displaying the words 'Soda Water, J. Young, Hibernian Works, Galway'. In larger print, beside the illustration, the advertisement urged: 'Ask for Young's Aerated Waters and support local industry. Manufactured at Hibernian Works, Galway.'

The jealousy grew even more absurd a few months later when, on a return visit to Dublin, Joyce was told by a treacherous former friend that Nora may not have been entirely faithful to him during their first few months together. He immediately challenged her severely in an anguished letter, but he then quickly reaffirmed his desire for her, irrespective of what she might have done 'with half the redheaded louts in the County Galway' (JJ to NB, 3 December 1909).

Three weeks later, a chance meeting in Dublin with a policeman who had known Nora in Galway, led to renewed jealousy and a plea: 'Forget everybody but me, darling. I am sure there are finer fellows in Galway than your poor lover but O, darling, one day you will see that I will be something in my country' (JJ to NB, 24 December 1909).

14 Cited in Maddox, *Nora*, p. 378.

15 DEASY: Deasy also engages Stephen about foot and mouth disease, which had not reached Ireland in 1904, but which was first found in Irish cattle in 1912, around the time that Joyce was in Galway. The disease was mentioned in the *Connacht Tribune* the week before he arrived in Galway (13 July 1912) and he mentions the

outbreak in a letter to Stanislaus from Galway (7 August) before referring to it again in two episodes of *Ulysses*.

16   HYDE: Douglas Hyde, the Roscommon-born founder of the Gaelic League and first president of Ireland, wrote poetry and plays in Irish under the pen name 'An Craoibhin Aoibhinn' ('the delightful little branch', or 'the pleasant little branch'). Hyde's *Love Songs of Connacht* was found in Joyce's Trieste library.

17   ARDILAUN: As well as being the chief narcotic of Dubliners in 1904, drink was also the killer of Paddy Dignam, whose funeral Bloom is preparing to attend. Joyce also used the word 'ardilaun' as a synonym for Guinness in *Finnegans Wake*, where there are multiple references to the Guinnesses, usually in the form of puns, including 'Ghinees hies good for you' (p. 16), 'Guinness thaw tool' (p. 35), 'Allfor Guineas' (p. 106), 'till Arthur comes againus' and 'Shares in guineases!' (p. 361), 'a bottle of ardilaun' (p. 407), 'Genghis is ghoon for you' (p. 593), 'Uncle Arth' (p. 608) and 'Archtur guiddus!' (p. 621).

Speculation that the Maamtrasna murders of 1882 were an attempt to silence witnesses to the dumping in Lough Mask of the bodies of two of Lord Ardilaun's bailiffs who had been murdered at the beginning of that year have been discounted (See Waldron, *Maamtrasna: The Murders and the Mystery* and Harrington, *The Maamtrasna Massacre: Impeachment of the Trials*). And an assertion by Padraic O Laoi in his Nora Barnacle biography that the murder of the two bailiffs, Joseph Huddy and his grandson John Huddy, happened on Thursday, 2 February 1882 – the day James Joyce was born – is erroneous. The men were murdered at the beginning of January and their bodies were recovered from Lough Mask on Friday, 27 January, seven days before Joyce was born (*Galway Vindicator*, 28 January 1882). Timothy Harrington was a friend of James Joyce's father and, like him, an ardent Parnellite. He was elected Lord Mayor of Dublin in 1901 and in that capacity he wrote a reference for James Joyce when he was leaving Dublin for Paris for the first time.

18   BELLO: Bello is Bella Cohen, the brothel's 'massive whoremistress', transgendered (to use a word that may not have existed in 1904). Leopold Bloom in the same surreal episode also becomes briefly a 'new womanly man' (*Ulysses*, 15:1798–9).

19   Frank Harris' writings on Shakespeare are also mentioned in the note on 'The Dark Lady of the Sonnets' in the programme notes Joyce wrote for the English Players performances in Zurich in 1918 at the same time as Nora appeared in *Riders to the Sea*.

20   SHEEHY: Stanislaus recalled: 'The father was a member of Parliament, and the family consisted of two clever brothers and four clever sisters, one of them a really handsome girl. David Sheehy, the father, was a vigorous-looking man, who lived to be about ninety. I liked him, but my brother thought him pompous and inclined to lay down the law' (Joyce, *My Brother's Keeper*, p. 88).

21   TOFT'S: Toft's amusement arcade is still in business in Salthill. A member of the Toft family was elected Mayor of Galway in the 1970s.

22   JJ to CC, 4 October 1936.

23 Monaghan, *Joyce's Dublin Family.*

24 O'GORMAN: Email to author 17 December 2011. In the mail he also recalled: 'Kathleen worked in the bindery, and when they were busy an SOS went out for more helpers. Apparently Nora, who lived nearby, or at least was easily contactable, often helped out in busy times, but only temporarily.'

25 County Galway Libraries Committee minutes in Galway County Council Archives, Island House, Nuns' Island, Galway.

26 The County Galway Libraries Committee was not the only forum dominated by bishops. Academics outnumbered clergymen only slightly on the UCG Governing Body during most of the twentieth century. In the mid-century academic year of 1950–1 – the year of Nora Barnacle's death – the twenty-five-member Governing Body included eleven academics and nine clergymen, comprising the Catholic Archbishop of Tuam and the Catholic bishops of Galway, Killaloe, Clonfert, Achonry and Killala, as well as two parish priests. The 1970–1 Governing Body included five Catholic bishops: Archbishop Walsh of Tuam, Bishop Michael Browne of Galway (nominated by the Minister of Education), Bishop Harty of Killaloe (representing Clare County Council), Bishop Hanly of Elphin (representing Sligo County Council) and Bishop Fergus of Achonry (co-opted). Michael Browne was succeeded on the Governing Body by his successor as Bishop of Galway, Eamonn Casey, who was also nominated by the Minister for Education (University College Galway Calendar).

27 CENSORED: Anthony Burgess has recalled: 'As a schoolboy I sneaked the two-volume Odysses Press edition into England, cut up into sections and distributed all over my body' (Burgess, *Here Comes Everybody*, p. 83).

   A film adaptation of *Ulysses* made in Dublin in 1967 with an all-star Irish cast led by Milo O'Shea as Leopold Bloom won Academy Award, Golden Globe and BAFTA nominations, but it was denied a release certificate in Ireland by the film censor and the appeals board. The outright ban was renewed in 1974 and it was not lifted until the year 2000, when the film was given a 15 certificate by the censor, Sheamus Smith (a former staff photographer on the *Irish Press* newspaper).

28 County Galway Libraries Committee minutes in Galway County Council Archives, Island House, Nuns' Island.

29 Ibid.

30 In the preface to the 1925 revised edition Gwynn wrote: 'In English literature there are certain authors who may be classed as obligatory – and concerning whom total ignorance is a defect which one should blush for ... an attempt has therefore been made to put together a survey of the literature which should concern itself only with such authors as can be deemed in this manner essential.' Stephen Gwynn was also a Nationalist Member of Parliament for Galway city from 1908 to 1918 and he was a lieutenant in the Connaught Rangers during World War I. He was a prolific author and Joyce had one of his books, *To-day and To-morrow in Ireland*, in his

Trieste library, having reviewed it for the *Daily Express* in 1903. In the review Joyce said that Gwynn's literary criticisms were 'the least interesting' essays in the book.

31 Tolkien held the position of External Examiner to the English Department of the then-UCG between 1949 and 1959, during which time he revised and published *The Lord of the Rings* (UCG Calendars 1950-9).

32 Lorna Reynolds was appointed Professor of Modern English at UCG in 1966. 'She made an immediate impact, revitalizing the department,' said her *Irish Times* obituary (26 July 2003).

33 UCG Calendar 1967.

34 UCG Calendar 1969.

35 Kieran Hoare email to author, 28 November 2014.

36 Tom Kenny email to author, 9 February 2015.

37 Another distinguished visitor to Kennys Bookshop on High Street was a later Joyce biographer, Edna O'Brien. 'Joyce! Now there's a writer. Why a page of Joyce a day is like a transfusion!' she told Tom Kenny (*Galway Advertiser*, 1 November 2012). Galwegians might, however, have been less impressed by O'Brien's description of Nora Barnacle as 'a fairly illiterate Galway girl' or her claim that 'many have been baffled that a man of Joyce's daunting intellect chose and remained constant to this peasant woman' (O'Brien, *James Joyce*).

38 Jack Griffin conversation with the author's father, Michael Burke.

39 JJ to Michael Healy, 1 July 1935.

40 *Irish Times*, 10 January 2015.

41 Email to author, 9 February 2015.

42 JJ to AB, 15 October 1936.

Ken Monaghan claimed that *Ulysses* had been translated into over 100 languages (Monaghan, *Irish Times*, 15 November 2003). Kevin Birmingham's estimate is much lower, but it includes Arabic, Norwegian, Catalan and Malayalam and two different Chinese translations. Birmingham has also estimated that *Ulysses* still sell about 100,000 copies each year, generating, therefore, nearly one million new sales every decade.

A well-in-advance plan to stage a dramatisation from *Ulysses*, to be called Bloomsday, at the Dublin Theatre Festival in 1958 was abandoned when the main sponsor, Bord Fáilte, withdrew financial support, fearing 'serious public controversy' following the intervention of the Catholic Archbishop of Dublin, Charles McQuaid (*Irish Independent*, 20 April 1958).

A couple of mid-1970s graduates of UCG, Brian and Mary Pat O'Donnell, from Limerick and Salthill, respectively, made a present of a first edition of *Ulysses* that they bought for €42,500 in 2007 to one of their sons, Bruce, before or after he embarked on a creative writing course at NUIG, according to documents filed at the High Court in Dublin during the couple's bankruptcy proceedings (*Sunday Business Post* and *Mail on Sunday*, both 15 March 2015).

5 – Buck

1   Gogarty's own copy of *The Holy Office* was, he recalled, 'destroyed by the bandits who burned my house' (Gogarty, *Rolling Down the Lea*).

2   Gogarty, *As I Was Going Down Sackville Street*, p. 205.

3   Another sample couplet: 'If anyone thinks that I amen't divine| He'll get no free drinks when I'm making the wine.'

4   Colum, *Our Friend James Joyce*, p. 66.

In *Tumbling In The Hay*, Gogarty's barely disguised 1939 memoir of his student days, Gideon Ouseley and his overbearing mother are clearly the author and his own mother, despite the endnote stating that 'all the characters are fictitious'. Several other references to his mother and 'the aunt' appear in the work, which also corroborates Joyce's description in the 'Oxen of the Sun' episode of *Ulysses* of the bacchanalian vigils of medical staff, students and friends in the National Maternity Hospital (p. 183).

The 1901 census return, completed by Gogarty's mother, Margaret, as head of the household and widow, lists three children and two servants. Oliver St John is described as a medical student, aged twenty-two. There is no mention of 'the aunt'. Her name appears among the residents of a boarding house on nearby Gardiner St. 'My aunt, of course, says that nobody can afford to drink at all,' writes 'Gideon Ouseley' in Gogarty's *Tumbling In The Hay*.

John Oliver, a miller and baker, of Mainguard Street, Galway, appears on the List of Irish Shareholders in the Atlantic Royal Mail Steam Navigation Company Limited in Collins, *Transatlantic Triumph & Heroic Failure*.

5   Joyce called Gogarty 'Dr O.S. Jesus Gogarty' in a letter to his brother Stanislaus (31 August 1906).

6   O'Connor, *Oliver St John Gogarty*, p. 89. Joyce himself uses the word 'slavey' to describe a female domestic servant in the *Dubliners* story 'Two Gallants' and in *Ulysses*, Mulligan calls one of the servants, Ursula, a skivvy. The falling-out can only have been intensified when Joyce was told, on a return visit to Dublin in 1909, that Gogarty may have been in cahoots with another former friend who claimed, falsely, to have been with Nora several times during Joyce's courtship of her (JJ to SJ, 21 August 1909).

7   JJ to SJ, 4 August 1909.

8   Gogarty, *As I Was Going Down Sackville Street*, pp. 294–5.

9   Gogarty, *Rolling Down the Lea*, pp. 117–8.

10 See 'Then here's a health to Mulligan's aunt' by Harald Beck and 'The afflicted mother – two letters' by Terence Killeen, *James Joyce Online Notes* [website].

11 *FW*, p. 86.

12 *Rolling Down the Lea* was published in London in 1950 with a frontispiece note that said 'By request of the author this book is not for sale in the Republic of Ireland'; a gibe at the Irish Censorship of Publications Board, not at Joyce.

13   *Saturday Review of Literature*, 18 March 1950.

14   Ibid.

15   Denis Johnston in Ryan, *A Bash in The Tunnel*, p. 163.

16   Seán Lester Diary, DCU.

17   *Connacht Tribune*, 8 September 1928.

18   JJ to HSW, 20 September 1928.

19   Gogarty, *Rolling Down the Lea*.

20   Ibid.

21   Lady Gregory frequently dined with the Gogartys when in Dublin. She wrote in her journal on Monday, 19 February 1923: 'Yesterday I went to see G. Yeats just come from London. She had been round to see Mrs Gogarty with some message and had found her crying, having just seen in the papers that Renvyle had been burned down' (*Lady Gregory's Journals*, Vol. 1, p. 436).

22   From Gogarty, *Rolling Down the Lea*, p. 143.

6 – Rock

1   The Margaretta Rock, 1.75 miles southwest of Mutton Island Lighthouse, can be seen from Blackrock and Knocknacarra at very low tide and its unlit buoy is clearly visible in daylight from Salthill and Grattan Road. Its foghorn was familiar to the ears of Galway city dwellers until it was decommissisoned by the Commissioners of Irish Lights in 1977. It is named after a British warship, *HMS Margaretta*, which ran aground on it ninety years before the *Indian Empire* did likewise.

2   The population of Galway city halved in the half-century following the Famine, dropping from 23,695 in 1851 to 13,426 in 1901.

3   The geographical advantage was noted outside Galway too. *Thom's Directory*, published in London and Dublin, described Galway Bay for much of the nineteenth century as 'possessing great advantages for foreign trade, particularly to America'.

4   'Beautiful calm without a cloud, smooth sea, placid ...' muses Bloom at Sandymount Strand in between the two references in *Ulysses* to the *Indian Empire* grounding.

5   The contract to carry mail was prestigious and potentially lucrative. The *Titanic*, launched fifty-three years after the *Indian Empire* steamed into Galway Bay, was officially named *RMS Titanic*, the initial letters standing for Royal Mail Ship. Some 3,500 mailbags containing 200,000 letters and packages were lost when it sank.

The advertisement in the *Galway Vindicator and Connaught Advertiser* was more detailed than the one in the *Tuam Herald*. The additional information stated: 'A Liberal table will be kept for First and Second Class; and a Dietary, according to the Government Seals, for the Third Class Passengers, who will have to provide themselves with a Tin Plate, Quart Mug, Knife, Fork, Spoon and Water Can. Each First and Second Class adult Cabin Passenger is allowed 20 Cubic Feet of baggage, freight free. Third Class passengers are allowed 10 Cubic Feet of Luggage for each

Adult, freight free, and all passengers must attend to the proper Shipment of Luggage. The Second and third Class Passengers must provide their own Bedding. NB Passengers should make early application, as the berths are fast filling up.'

6   Galway city had three weekly newspapers in 1858: *The Galway Vindicator and Connaught Advertiser*, which appeared every Wednesday and Saturday; *The Galway Mercury* and *The Galway Express*, both published every Saturday. The *Tuam Herald* was, and still is, published every Saturday.

The *Tuam Herald* editorial also said: 'Until by some miraculous transposition of place, the Liverpool millionaires can shove Holyhead 300 miles to the West of its present position, Galway will possess its advantages. Money and its unscrupulous use may attempt to throw obstacles in the way, as it is reported to have done on former occasions. But in the end these tricks will come to exposure and bring to shame those who lend themselves to such unworthy proceedings.'

The *Galway Vindicator and Connaught Advertiser* had been much more cautious a week earlier when, on the day of the grounding, it reported that the *Indian Empire* had suffered 'a slight accident' on entering the harbour, 'which, as it is at present the subject of judicial investigations, we do not deem it right to advert to at any length'.

7   The inner bay pilots in 1858 were Joseph Evans and Bartholomew Oliver (*Thom's*).

8   Fr Peter Daly had been a Galway town commissioner since 1844 and a harbour commissioner, elected for life, since 1849. Although he never formally served as chairman of the Harbour Commissioners, he sometimes chaired their meetings in the absence of the incumbent. According to the Galway historian and academic Dr John Cunningham, Fr Daly was 'the dominant public figure in Galway during the 1850s' and 'a stubborn, abrasive, guileful and egotistical populist' (*Galway 1790–1914: A Town Tormented by the Sea*, p. 166). Fr Daly was ordained in 1815 and appointed Parish Priest of St Nicholas's Parish in the centre of Galway three years later. He was responsible for bringing the Sisters of Charity and the Sisters of Mercy to Galway and he ran soup kitchens during the Famine. He was heavily involved in the successful campaign to bring the railway to Galway. He laid the foundation stone of O'Brien's Bridge in 1851 and he relocated the Lynch Window on Market Street. He was praised in an Anthony Raftery poem for breaking up a proselytizing meeting in Loughrea. A head-and-shoulders bust of him stands in Bushy Park Catholic Church, in whose grounds he is buried.

9   The funding application was supported in the House of Commons by the other Galway MP, William Gregory of Coole Park, the future husband of Lady Augusta Gregory, but he did not buy shares in the line and he did not sail on its vessels when he crossed the Atlantic twice in 1859 to visit Canada and the United States.

10   The Galway Harbour Commissioners' records stored on microfilm at the James Hardiman Library at NUIG contain only brief minutes of a meeting on 16 June 1858, but no reference to the special meeting on the *Indian Empire* grounding on that date. Anthony O'Flaherty and Pierce Joyce later became chairmen of the Galway Harbour Commissioners.

11 'Joyce is attracted to sensational criminal cases which remained unresolved,' noted Anne Fogarty in *Voices on Joyce*.
12 French, *The Book As World: James Joyce's Ulysses*, pp. 214–15.
13 JJ to Frank Budgen, 28 February 1921.
14 Hardiman source is: 'Suspecting, proving, knowing: Three cases of unnatural death in Joyce's *Ulysses*' in Fogarty and O'Rourke, *Voices on Joyce*.

7 – Aughrim

1 Curran, *James Joyce Remembered*, p. 41.
2 *Irish Press*, 14 January 1941.
3 Power, *Conversations with James Joyce*, p. 54.
4 See Hugh Shields, 'The History of "The Lass of Aughrim"', *Irish Musical Studies 1: Musicology in Ireland*, Irish Academic Press, 1990, and 'The Dead Lass of Aughrim' by George L. Geckle in *Eire/Ireland*, Fomhar 1974, pp. 86–96.
5 The versions known to Joyce and the Barnacles are not written down. Both recent versions, and regional variations of them, say 'yellow locks' where Joyce wrote 'heavy locks'. (Joyce may have replaced 'yellow' with 'heavy' merely to show that the self-regarding Bartell D'Arcy did not know the words of the song fully.)
6 Shovlin, *Journey Westward*. Shovlin is not alone is suggesting that the Gregory allusion is deliberate and that memories of the Famine pervade 'The Dead'. Historian Kevin Whelan has written that 'the buried history of the Famine [is] embedded' at the centre of the story and is its primary theme. He suggested that 'the association of the Gregory family with Galway' may have been the reason that the imported Scottish ballad evolved into 'The Lass of Aughrim', 'a folk song which summoned the deep, oral, Irish-language, Jacobite, Gaelic past of the west of Ireland'. Whelan also noted that the story 'insistently emphasizes food and hospitality' and that Joyce had told his brother Stanislaus that 'The Dead' was 'a ghost story' (see 'The Memories of "The Dead"', *The Yale Journal of Criticism*, Spring 2002). Whelan also argued in the same article that Joyce's use of snow 'falling softly' and 'softly falling' in 'The Dead' was influenced by a passage in George Moore's 1886 novel *A Drama in Muslin*, which is set partly in Galway, around Gort, Kinvara, Ardrahan and 'Dungory Castle'. More recently, Robert Smart, of Quinnipiac University, has proposed that 'the lonely churchyard on the hill' in the last paragraph of 'The Dead' is undoubtedly a Famine reference. 'Post-Famine,' he wrote, 'the mention of any desolate, wasted landscape in any Irish text becomes a Famine reference, an indication of how powerful this moment in modern Irish history became' (see Smart, *Black Roads: The Famine in Irish Literature*).
7 See Kelly, *The Graves Are Walking*, p. 250.
8 O'Rourke, *The History of the Great Irish Famine*, pp. 330–3.
9 Jenkins, *Sir William Gregory of Coole*, p. 72.

10 Ibid., p. 75.

11 Augusta Gregory, *Autobiography of the Right Honourable Sir William Gregory* (London, 1894), cited in Fahy, *Kiltartan: Many Leaves One Root*.

12 Fahy, *Kiltartan: Many Leaves One Root*, p. 163.

13 Ibid., p. 164.

14 Breatnach, *Kinvara: A Seaport town on Galway Bay*.

15 *Tuam Herald*, 8 December 1849 (cited in Fahy, *Kiltartan: Many Leaves One Root*).

16 Jenkins, *Sir William Gregory of Coole*, p. 108.

Fifty years after the Famine, Lady Gregory herself wrote: 'We have no evicted tenants in this neighbourhood ... we are still on good terms with our people' (*Seventy Years*, p. 265).

Sir William also paid for the restoration of the round tower at Kilmacduagh, a little south of Gort. It is the tallest round tower in Ireland and it is still intact. And he built Kiltartan National School, which still stands and is preserved as the Kiltartan Gregory Museum, at Kiltartan Cross. He had inherited some 15,000 acres around Coole, stretching from Gort in the south to Ardrahan in the north and including the seaport village of Kinvara and surrounding lands, but by 1857 gambling debts and inherited mortgages had forced him to sell off all but 5,000 acres surrounding Coole Park.

17 He proposed to her in a letter in which he acknowledged, but understated, that she was young enough to be his daughter. Coole Park is 7 miles from Roxborough House.

18 Pethica and Roy, *To the Land of the Free from this Island of Slaves: Henry Stratford Persse's Letters from Galway to America, 1821–1832*, pp. 3, 9, 16, 57.

19 The cut-stone distillery building, to which Henry Stratford Persse moved the enterprise from its initial location further up the Corrib at Newcastle, is still prominent, though derelict, on Nuns' Island, opposite Bowling Green. It is now owned by NUI Galway, as is the original site at Newcastle.

20 List of Irish Shareholders in the Atlantic Royal Mail Steam Navigation Company Limited in Collins, *Transatlantic Triumph & Heroic Failure*.

21 In December 1899, she wrote in her diary: 'I spent my time alone chiefly in collecting materials for an account of Raftery. I found his place of burial at Killeenan, and borrowed a MSS book of his poems, and went to the lodge by moonlight each evening to translate them with Mulkere's help; and then wrote my article' (Gregory, *Seventy Years*, p. 343).

Despite her close and enduring friendship with William Butler Yeats, Lady Gregory acknowledged in a 1924 article on Connacht poets that 'for a hundred years Raftery, who wandered blind and homeless through Connacht, has been given "the branch", the greater praise of the people'. She conceded that Raftery's verses had praised most highly places in County Mayo, where he was born and lived until smallpox blinded him in childhood, but she pointed out that one of his songs was 'Le Taoibh Chiltartain' (beside Kiltartan). And she added: 'I was well pleased when an old woman said to me: "I used often to see him when I was a little child in my father's house at Corker, and here at Coole House he used to be as well'" (*Connacht Tribune*, 15 March 1924). Twenty-five years earlier, she had outlined how she had searched for and found Raftery's previously unmarked grave and arranged for a headstone to be placed over it. She hired a local stonecutter to carve an upright slab with a Celtic cross and only the word Raftery (in Irish) on it. 'The old man who buried him (65 years earlier) was sad because his other name, "Anthony", had not been given, but he was comforted with the thought that Homer also is known by no second name,' she recalled (*An Claidheamh Soluis*, 8 September 1900).

22 Gregory, *Seventy Years*, p. 363.

23 The 2016 equivalent income or purchasing power of £5.00 Sterling in 1904 would be about €380, according to MeasuringWorth.com, a website overseen by economists from universities in Britain and the USA.

24 In asking Yeats to help Joyce in 1902, Lady Gregory had written: 'I think he has genius of a kind and I like his pride and waywardness. I have written to a friend in Paris about him ... Joyce's father is too poor and I think Joyce can only gather up money together to pay his fare over and keep him for two or three weeks ... I hope he will be alright. The more I know him the better I like him, and though I wish he could remain in Ireland still I would like to see him prosper somewhere. I am sure he will make a name somewhere ... poor boy, I am afraid he will knock his ribs against the earth, but he has grit and will succeed in the end' (Gregory, *Seventy Years*, pp. 425–6).

25 JJ to mother, 20 March 1903.

26 Joyce, *My Brother's Keeper*, p. 193.

27 JJ in his 1901 essay 'The Day of the Rabblement', reprinted in Barry, *James Joyce: Occasional, Critical and Political Writing*, p. 50.

28 Gregory, *Poets and Dreamers*, p. 196.

29 Ibid., p. 196.

30 Joyce, *My Brother's Keeper*, p. 54.

31 Limerick reference is in *The Journals*, Vol. 2, p. 270.

32 Aside from Lady Gregory, the other Irish writers who signed the letter were: Brinsley MacNamara, Seán O'Casey, Liam O'Flaherty, Seamus O'Sullivan, Lennox Robinson, George Russell, James Stephens and W. B. Yeats.

33 Lady Gregory, *Coole*, p. 50.

34 *FW*, p. 340.

35 Shovlin, *Journey Westward*, p. 91.

36 Shovlin, *Journey Westward*, p. 94.

37 John Huston became an Irish citizen in 1964.

38 *Sunday Tribune*, 10 January 1999.

39 *Sunday Independent*, 19 July 2009.

40 *Irish Independent*, 23 November 2010.

41 NUIG Press Release, 22 November 2010.

42 *Irish Independent*, 23 November 2010. The poet Paul Muldoon (a performer at the first Galway Arts Festival in 1977) recalls in a 1987 poem his delight at hearing the strains of 'The Lass of Aughrim' performed on a flute while he was boating on a tributary of the Amazon (Muldoon, 'The Lass of Aughrim', *Meeting The British*).

The Dead was released by Liffey Films in 1987.

Did Joyce, an incurable data collector, base the exchanges about goloshes between Gretta and Gabriel's aunts in 'The Dead' on a conversation he had had with William Butler Yeats? Lady Gregory has recalled: 'I went to see Yeats who had been coughing terribly yesterday. He said Symons, who had dined with him the night before, had discussed the question as to whether any man with self-respect could wear goloshes, as he, like Yeats, arrives at the house he dines in with muddy boots' (Gregory, *Seventy Years*, p. 357).

8 – *Lucia*

1 The Galway Workhouse 'in practice became the hospital for the city poor', wrote Dr James P. Murray in *Galway: A Medico Social History* (Kennys, 1994). He added: 'The Lying-in [maternity] ward was never popular and was shunned by "respectable" women.'

2 Burgess, *Here Comes Everybody*, p. 30.

3 *Daily Telegraph*, 27 September 1932, cited in Shloss, *Lucia Joyce: To Dance in the Wake*, p. 245.

4 Ellmann, *James Joyce*, p. 545.

5 JJ to HSW, 9 June 1936.

6 Ibid.

7 Joyce's letter – handwritten in green ink – can be read in the Dublin City University Historical Collections Research Centre.

8 Seán Lester Diary, DCU.

9 Ibid.

10 Evelyn Cotton to HSW, 18 June 1947, in British Library.

11 JJ to Mrs Eileen Joyce Schaurek, 13 March 1935.

12 Schloss, *Lucia Joyce: To Dance in the Wake*, pp. 409, 417.

13 *Pomes Penyeach* papers, NUIG.

14 Ibid.

15 Affidavit in Kathleen Barnacle papers, NUIG.

16 JJ to Con Curran, 4 Oct 1936.

17 JJ to NB, 31 August 1909.

18 Joyce, *Ulysses*, p. 101 and Slote, *Ulysses: Annotated*, 465.

19 It is also the church where Oliver St John Gogarty's mother attended sodality evenings and novenas in *Tumbling In The Hay*.

20 Bach, Dvorak, Haydn, Kodaly, Liszt, Pergolesi and Vivaldi are among many other composers who have created musical versions of the *Stabat Mater* (see Fisher, *Stabat Mater: The Mystery Hymn*).

21 To borrow the words used in another context by Bob Dylan.

9 – Zurich

1 In *The Odyssey*, by Homer, Tiresias tell Odysseus during his visit to Hades: 'At the last, amidst a happy folk, shall your own death come to you, softly, far from the salt sea, and make an end of one utterly weary of slipping downward into old age.' And Joyce foretold his own death in *Ulysses* when the ghost of Stephen's mother appears and reminds him: 'All must go through it, Stephen ... You too. Time will come' (Slote, *Ulysses: Annotated,* 408). He also wrote in *Finnegans Wake*, in the final lines of his final work: 'I am passing out. O bitter ending! I'll slip away before they're up. They'll never see. Nor know. Nor miss me. And it's old and old it's sad and old it's sad and weary I go back to you, my cold father, my cold mad father, my cold mad feary father, till the near sight of the mere size of him, the moyles and moyles of it, moananoaning, makes me seasilt saltsick and I rush, my only, into your arms ...'

2 'The afflicted mother' who is mentioned in *Ulysses* is clearly Stephen's mother, not Gogarty's. 'Jesus meets his afflicted mother' is the Fourth Station of the Cross in Catholic churches, the fourth pause on Mary's *Via Dolorosa* leading to the crucifixion.

3 Seán Lester Diary for 16 December 1940, DCU Library Historical Collections Research Centre and also O'Connor, *The Joyce We Knew*.

4 The family arrived in Zurich on 17 December 1940, after an exhausting and tension-filled journey. Nora told Lester in Geneva two days earlier that 'Zurich had always been associated with certain crises in their life: they had rushed from Austria at the beginning of the last war and had lived in Zurich very comfortably; they had spent their honeymoon there; it was there that Joyce's eyesight had been saved and now they were going back in another crisis' (Seán Lester Diary, 16 December 1940, DCU).

5 The front page of the *Connacht Sentinel* that recorded Joyce's death – Tuesday, 14 January 1941 – was dominated by news of World War II, but it also reported that Galway County Council's finance committee had agreed on the previous Saturday – the day after Joyce entered hospital – that it would sell the site of Galway Prison where Myles Joyce was hanged in 1882 for the Maamtrasna murders. It was sold to the Catholic Bishop, Dr Michael Browne, 'for the nominal sum of 10 pounds' so that a cathedral could be built there for the diocese. The report added that the committee agreed that, instead of inserting a clause in the deed, it would accept an undertaking from the bishop that the site would revert back to the County Council

'if the proposed cathedral is not raised to a height of 12 feet on the site within the lifetime of three priests whose names are given and 21 years thereafter'.

6   Carola Giedion-Weckler to Lester in Lester Diaries at DCU.

7   Orfeo (Orpheus), refusing to accept Eurydice's death, pledges to follow her to the Underworld. He sings: 'You are dead, my life, and I still breathe? | You are gone from me | Never to return, and I should remain? | No, for if verses can do anything, | I will go in safety to the deepest abysses, | And having softened the heart of the King of shades, | I will bring you back with me to see the stars again: | Oh, if wicked destiny refuses me this, | I will stay with you, in the company of death, | Farewell earth, farewell Heaven and Sun, farewell' (Translated by Gilbert Blin for the Boston Early Music Festival 2012. See bemf.org).

8   Potts, *Portraits of the Artist in Exile*.

9   Ibid.

10 GJ to HSW, 18 March 1941 in British Library.

11 *Irish Times*, 21 November 1949.

12 Gilbert, *Introduction to Letters of James Joyce*.

13 Power, *Conversations with JJ*, p. 89.

14 Kathleen Barnacle papers, NUIG.

15 Ibid.

16 NB to HSW, 22 September 1943 in British Library.

17 Ibid.

18 *Irish Times*, 12 November 1949.

19 Ibid.

20 Evelyn Cotton to HSW, 27 August 1947 in British Library. Nora's anger over the Léon papers may also explain why the *Finnegans Wake* material was donated to the British Library, not the National Library of Ireland.

21 Colum, *Our Friend James Joyce*, p. 238.

22 JJ to NB, 1 November 1909.

23 Colum, *Our Friend James Joyce*, p. 238.

24 Undated letter in HSW documents in the British Library.

25 JJ to NB, 22 December 1909.

26 JJ to NB, 1 November 1909.

27 Giorgio's telegram to HSW, 10 April 1951, in the HSW papers in the British Library.

28 Ellmann, Introduction to *Selected Letters*, 1957.

29 Tentative talk about repatriation of Joyce's body led nowhere. The Minister for External Affairs, Seán Mac Bride, wrote to Nora in the late 1940s to say that the Irish government would be proud to claim Joyce. In the 1970s Taoiseach Jack Lynch agreed that a naval corvette would bring the body home for burial 'with full State honours', if Joyce's son and grandson agreed, according to Ulick O'Connor (*Sunday Independent*, 30 January 2011).

30 Molly Bloom's soliloquy, written more than thirty years before Nora's death,

includes: '[E]very day I get up theres some new thing on sweet God sweet God well when Im stretched out dead in my grave I suppose Ill have some peace ...'

31 JJ to NB, 22 December 1909.
32 Ibid.

BIBLIOGRAPHY

Barry, Kevin (Ed.), *James Joyce: Occasional, Critical, and Political Writing* (Oxford: Oxford University Press, 2000)

Barry, Kevin, *The Dead* (Cork: Cork University Press, 2011)

Birmingham, Kevin, *The Most Dangerous Book* (London: Head of Zeus, 2014)

Breatnach, Caoilte, *Kinvara: A Seaport Town on Galway Bay* (Kinvara: Tír Eolas, 1997)

Burgess, Anthony, *Here Comes Everybody* (London: Arena, 1987)

Collins, Timothy, *Transatlantic Triumph & Heroic Failure: The Galway Line* (Cork: The Collins Press, 2002)

Colum, Mary and Padraic, *Our Friend James Joyce* (London: Victor Gollancz Limited, 1959)

Costello, Peter, *James Joyce: The Years of Growth 1882–1915* (Schull: Roberts Rinehart Publishers, 1992)

Costello, Peter and John Wyse Jackson, *John Stanislaus Joyce* (New York: St Martin's Press, 1998)

Cunningham, Dr John, *Galway 1790–1914: A Town Tormented by the Sea* (Dublin: Geography Publications, 2004)

Curran, C.P., *James Joyce Remembered* (New York and London: Oxford University Press, 1968)

Douglas, Ken, *The Downfall of the Spanish Armada in Ireland* (Dublin, Gill and Macmillan, 2009)

Ellmann, Richard, *James Joyce* (Oxford: Oxford University Press, 1982)

Ellmann, Richard (Ed.), *James Joyce: Poems and Shorter Writings* (London: Faber and Faber, 1991)

Ellmann, Richard, *Selected Letters of James Joyce* (London: Faber and Faber, 1975)

Ellmann, Richard, *Ulysses On The Liffey* (London: Faber and Faber, 1972)

Fahy, Mary de Lourdes, *Kiltartan: Many Leaves One Root* (Kiltartan: The Kiltartan Gregory Cultural Society, 2004)

Fisher, Desmond, *Stabat Mater: The Mystery Hymn* (Leominster, UK: Gracewing, 2015)

Fitzgerald, Robert (Trans.), *The Odyssey* (London: Vintage Books, 2007)

Foley, Tadhg, *From Queen's College to National University* (Dublin: Four Courts Press, 1999)

French, Marilyn, *The Book As World: James Joyce's Ulysses* (London: Abacus, 1982)

Gilbert, Stuart, *Letters of James Joyce* (New York: The Viking Press, 1957)

Gogarty, Oliver St John, *As I Was Going Down Sackville Street* (London: Sphere Books, 1968)

Gogarty, Oliver St John, *Rolling Down the Lea* (London: Constable and Company Ltd, 1950)

Gogarty, Oliver St John, *Tumbling in the Hay* (London: Constable, 1939)

Gorman, Herbert, *James Joyce* (New York: Rinehart & Company, Inc, 1939)

Gregory, Lady Augusta, *Coole* (Dublin: Cuala Press, 1931)

Gregory, Lady Augusta, *Poets and Dreamers* (New York: Kennikat Press Inc., 1967)

Gregory, Lady Augusta, *Seventy Years* (New York: Macmillan Publishing Co., Inc., 1974)

Gregory, Lady Augusta, *The Journals* (Gerrards Cross, UK: Colin Smythe Limited, 1978)

Gwynn, Stephen, *The Masters of English Literature* (London: Macmillan and Co. Ltd, 1931)

Hardiman, James, *The History of the Town and County of the Town of Galway* (Galway: Connacht Tribune (reprint), 1926)

Harrington, Timothy, *Maamtrasna Massacre: Impeachment of the Trials* (Dublin: Nation Office, 1884)

Hart-Davis, Duff, *Armada* (London: Bantam Press, 1988)

Huston, Anjelica, *A Story Lately Told* (London: Simon & Schuster UK, 2014)

Huston, Anjelica, *Watch Me* (London: Simon & Schuster UK, 2015)

Igoe, Vivien, *James Joyce's Dublin Houses* (Dublin: Wolfhound Press, 1997)

Jenkins, Brian, *Sir William Gregory of Coole* (Gerrards Cross, UK: Colin Smythe Limited, 1986)

Joyce, James, *Finnegans Wake* (Ware, UK: Wordsworth Classics, 2012)

Joyce, James, *Stephen Hero* (London: Panther Books, 1977)

Joyce, James, *Ulysses* (London: The Bodley Head, 1960)

Joyce, Stanislaus, *My Brother's Keeper* (London: Faber and Faber, 1958)

Kelly, John, *The Graves Are Walking* (London: Faber and Faber, 2012)

Levin, Harry, *A James Joyce Reader* (London: Penguin Books, 1993)

Levin, Harry, *James Joyce* (New York: New Directions Publishing Corporation, 1960)

Lynd, Robert, *Galway of the Races: Selected Essays* (Dublin: The Lilliput Press, 1990)

Lyons, J.B., *Oliver St John Gogarty* (Dublin: The Blackwater Press, 1980)

McCourt, John, *The Years of Bloom* (Dublin: The Lilliput Press, 2001)

McCourt, John, *James Joyce: A Passionate Exile* (London: Orion Books Ltd, 2000)

McGuinness, Frank, *The Dead: A Dramatization* (London: Faber and Faber, 2012)

Maddox, Brenda, *Nora: The Real Life of Molly Bloom* (Boston: Houghton Mifflin Company, 1988)

Meaney, Gerardine, *Nora* (Cork: Cork University Press, 2004)

Monaghan, Ken, *Joyce's Dublin Family* (Dublin: The James Joyce Centre, 2005)

Muldoon, Paul, *Meeting The British* (Faber and Faber, 1987)

Murray, James P., *Galway: A Medico-Social History* (Galway: Kennys, 1994)

Nicholson, Adam, *The Mighty Dead: Why Homer Matters* (London, William Collins, 2014)

Nicholson, Robert, *The Ulysses Guide* (Dublin: New Island Books, 1988)

Norris, Margot, *Ulysses* (Cork: Cork University Press, 2004)

O'Brien, Edna, *James Joyce* (London: Weidenfeld & Nicholson, 1999)

O'Connor, Ulick, *Oliver St John Gogarty* (St Albans: Granada Publishing Limited, 1981)

O'Connor, Ulick (Ed.), *The Joyce We Knew* (Kerry: Brandon, 2004)

Ó Domhnaill, Rónán Gearóid, *Gone the Way of Truth: Historic Graves of Galway* (Dublin: The History Press, 2016)

O'Donoghue, Fergus, SJ (Ed.), *Studies: Celebrating James Joyce* (Dublin: 2014)

O Laoi, Padraic, *Nora Barnacle Joyce: A Portrait* (Galway: Kennys, 1982)

O'Neill, T.P., *The Tribes and Other Galway Families* (Galway: Connacht Tribune Ltd, 1984)

O'Rourke, Rev. John, *The History of the Great Irish Famine* (Maynooth: 1874)

Pethica, James L. and Roy C., James (Eds), *To the Land of the Free from this Island of Slaves: Henry Stratford Persse's Letters from Galway to America, 1821–1832* (Cork: Cork University Press, 1998)

Potts, William (Ed.), *Portraits of the Artist in Exile* (Seattle: University of Washington Press, 1979)

Power, Arthur, *Conversations with James Joyce* (Dublin: The Lilliput Press, 1999)

Rafter, Kevin (Ed.), *Irish Journalism Before Independence: More a Disease than a Profession* (Manchester: Manchester University Press, 2011)

Ryan, John (Ed.) *A Bash In The Tunnel* (London: Clifton Books, 1970)

Saddlemyer, Ann and Smythe, Colin (Eds), *Lady Gregory: Fifty Years After* (Gerrards Cross, UK: Colin Smythe Limited, 1987)

Shloss, Carol Loeb, *Lucia Joyce: To Dance in the Wake* (London: Bloomsbury edition, 2005)

Shovlin, Frank, *Journey Westward* (Liverpool: Liverpool University Press, 2014)

Slote, Sam, *Ulysses: Annotated* (Richmond, UK: Alma Classics, 2012)

Smart, Robert, *Black Roads: The Famine in Irish Literature* (Hamden, USA: Quinnipiac University Press, 2015)

Tindall, William York, *The Joyce Country* (New York: Schocken Books, 1972)

Tóibín, Colm, *Lady Gregory's Toothbrush* (London: Picador, 2003)

Waldron, Jarlath, *Maamtrasna: The Murders and the Mystery* (Dublin: Edmund Burke Publisher, 1992)

Woodman, Kieran, *Safe and Commodious: The Annals of the Galway Harbour Commissioners, 1830–1997* (Galway: Galway Harbour Company, 2000)